THE
FOOTBALL
REVOLUTION

THE
FOOTBALL
REVOLUTION

*A Study of the Changing Pattern of
Association Football*

By
George W. Keeton
MA, LLD, FBA

ISBN 0 7153 5688 7

84599
JP| 7 96.334 09

Set in 11/13pt Plantin
and printed in Great Britain
by W J Holman Limited Dawlish Devon
for David & Charles (Publishers) Limited
South Devon House   Newton Abbot   Devon

Contents

List of Illustrations

I

The Evolution of Association Football

No-one knows when and where football was first played. It was certainly popular, especially in England and Italy in the early middle ages, but its only resemblance to the modern game was that a large ball was used. There was no limit to the number of contestants, and any means of propelling the ball was permitted. Significantly, the game—if game it can be called—often served as an outlet for the rivalries of adjoining towns or villages. The entire able-bodied male population of the two villages turned out in an effort to kick or carry the ball from one village to the other. When this was achieved, the game ended, but by that time the list of casualties was high and some of them might be fatal. There are survivals of this primitive form even today in northern Italy and northern England, although it has now been formalised, and casualties are few and rarely serious.

There is plenty of evidence of the popularity of this sport in England from the middle ages onwards, for legislation frequently attempted to check it, always without success. Thus, in an instruction to the Lord Lieutenant of Kent (along with other Lords Lieutenant) in 1363, King Edward III writes:

> Whereas the people of our realm, rich and poor alike were accustomed formerly in their games to practise archery—whence by God's help it is well-known that high honour and profit came to our realm, and no small advantage to ourselves in our warlike enterprises—and that now skill in the use of the bow having fallen almost wholly into disrepute, our subjects give themselves up to the throwing of stones and of wood and of iron; and some to handball and football and hockey; and others to coursing and cockfights, and even to other unseemly sports less useful and

manly; whereby our realm—which God forbid—will soon, it would appear, be void of archers.

We, wishing that a fitting remedy be found in this matter, do hereby ordain, that in all places in your county, liberties or no liberties, wheresoever you shall deem fit, a proclamation be made to this effect: that every man in the same county, if he be able-bodied, shall, upon holidays, make use, in his games, of bows and arrows, and so learn and practise archery.

Moreover, we ordain that you prohibit under penalty of imprisonment all and sundry from such stone, wood and iron throwing; handball, football or hockey; courting and cockfighting; or other such idle games.

It was all to no avail. The Englishman continued to play his traditional games, ignoring this and other laws. Sir Thomas Elyot, in his *Castle of Health*, written in the reign of Henry VIII, mentions football among popular sports and exercises beneficial to health, but his view is a good deal more benevolent than that of an Elizabethan writer, Stubbes, who in his *Anatomy of Abuses* published in 1583, writes:

As concerning football playing, I protest now to you it may rather be called a friendly kind of fight than a play or recreation; a bloody and murthering practice, than a fellowly sport or pastime. For dooth not every one lye in waight for his adversarie, seeking to overthrowe him and to picke (ie, pitch) him on his nose, though it be upon hard stones, in ditch or dale, in valley or hill, or what place so-ever it be, hee careth not, so he have him down. And he that can serve most of this fashion, he is counted the only fellow; and who but he? So that by this means, sometimes their necks are broken, sometimes their backs, sometimes their legs, sometime their armes; sometime one part thrust out of joint, sometime another; sometime the noses gush out with blood, sometime their eyes start out, and sometimes hurt in one place, sometimes in another. But whosoever scapeth away the best, goeth not scot free, but is either sore wounded, craised, and brused, so as he dyeth of it, or else scapeth very hardly. And no mervaile, for they have the sleights to meet one betwixt two, to dashe him against the hart with their elbowes, to hit him under the short ribs with their griped fists, and with their knees to catch him upon the hip, and to pick (pitch) him on his nose, with a hundred such murdering devices; and hereof groweth envy, malice, rancour, choler, hatred, displeasure, enmitie, and what not else; and sometimes fighting, brawling, contention, quarrel-picking, murther, homicide, and great effusion of blood, as experience daly teacheth.

Is this murthering play now, an exercise for the Sabath day? Is this a Christian dealing, for one brother to mayme and hurt another, and that upon prepensed malice or set purpose? Is this to do to another as we would wish another to do to us? God make us more careful over the bodyes of our brethren!

The picture may have been exaggerated, but it cannot be denied that the sport was only for tough men. Stubbes expresses the reaction of Puritans to it, and it is not surprising that, along with other sports and pastimes, it was rigidly suppressed during the Commonwealth, and the unpopularity of these measures was one of the factors leading to the Restoration.

Football retained its popularity throughout the eighteenth century, and it had now found a permanent home in the public schools. It was at Westminster that the poet Cowper was outstanding at football for no less than eight years (1741-9). Each school had its own rules, and there was the very widest variation in fields of play, and even of the numbers of those taking part. This variety prevented the game from becoming more than a domestic pastime of the school. At this date, practically all sets of rules allowed handling in some degree, and games called for courage rather than skill—as is apparent from the graphic description of the game at Rugby given by Thomas Hughes in *Tom Brown's Schooldays*. Clearly the author had himself experienced all that is there described.

In spite of the very wide variation in rules, the game of football increased rapidly in popularity in the mid-nineteenth century, and a few years later old boys' clubs kept together those who had played together at school. It is during this period that the Old Etonians, the Old Carthusians, the Old Harrovians, and other Old Boys' clubs were formed. These, with the Royal Engineers, one of several Army clubs, were to dominate the early years of cup-fighting. After one or two abortive attempts to agree upon a set of rules which might be acceptable to all, a meeting was called at the Freemasons' Tavern, in Great Queen Street, in October 1863, for the purpose of establishing a representative body, whose rules should be binding upon all clubs. The meeting was somewhat casually attended, and there were no representatives of the schools, but out of it there emerged the Football Association.

It at once found itself faced with major difficulties. One was agreement upon the code of laws which governed play. There was sharp division between those who would permit handling, and those who did not. The argument continued for over ten years, and ultimately the handlers, led by Blackheath, whose captain and secretary had attended the meeting at the Freemasons' Tavern, seceded to found the Rugby Union.

The second difficulty arose from the attitude of the public schools, who remained firmly attached to their own codes. Their attitude only altered when the Association had established its position in the country as a whole. In the early years, it was not without rivals. The Sheffield Association had been formed in 1867 in an area where there were already a number of clubs. They played under a code which had a closer resemblance to that of modern football than the first rules of the Football Association itself. In 1868 Sheffield and London played the first of a long succession of games between the two cities, and a way to a union of the two Associations was opened.

For its hard-won successes in these early years, the Football Association owed much to the enthusiasm and ability of C. A. Alcock, one of the outstanding players of this period, whose abilities on the field of play for the famous Wanderers were matched by organising abilities of the highest order. Elected a committee member in 1866, he became secretary in 1870, the year in which a joint team from Sheffield and London played a Scottish team. This match has some claim to be regarded as the first international match.

In October 1871, a decisive step forward was taken when it was decided to institute a knock-out 'Challenge' Competition for a cup. The first trophy cost £20, and was made and designed by Martin & Halls, of Sheffield, although surprisingly there were no entries from that city in the first season. Perhaps they felt that travelling expenses would be too heavy, for although a Scottish side, the famous Queen's Park, were amongst the first contestants, they were excused until the semi-final, and when in that game, played in London, they drew with the Wanderers, they had no money to cover the expenses of a second game and therefore conceded the tie to the Wanderers, who went on to beat the Royal Engineers by a single goal. The Wanderers were, of course, led by Alcock himself, but among the Royal Engineers (whose team consisted entirely of officers) was Col Sir Francis Marindin, who was to be an able president of the Football Association in its earliest, and purely amateur period.

Another of the early pioneers who decisively influenced the development of the game was Lord Kinnaird, who played for the Wanderers, the Old Etonians and for Sheffield. He also played in no less than nine Cup Finals.

Looking back, it is evident that the game was fortunate in attracting the energies of so many really able administrators, over long periods of time. For a period of nearly a century, the Association had only three secretaries—C. W. Alcock, from 1870 until 1894, Sir Frederick Wall from 1894 until 1934 (a period in which the game reached maturity), and Sir Stanley Rous from 1934 until 1962. When Sir Stanley retired from the secretaryship of the Football Association it was to become president of the international organisation, FIFA (Federation International de Football Association), in the creation of which he had played a leading part. It was largely as a result of his initiative that the national associations of the United Kingdom, and the clubs within their jurisdictions, have entered fully into European, and ultimately world competitions, transforming the character of the game in consequence.

For the first Cup competition in the 1871-2 season, fifteen clubs entered. They were Barnes, Civil Service, Clapham Rovers, Hitchin, Maidenhead, Marlow, Queen's Park (from Glasgow), Donington School, Hampstead Heathens, Harrow Chequers,

Reigate Priory, Royal Engineers, Upton Park, Crystal Palace, and the Wanderers. Possibly one of the most remarkable features of this entry is that, after the lapse of a century, some of these clubs still enter year by year for this first of all football competitions.

There can be no question of the unifying effect of this competition, nor of its popularity. Nearly two thousand spectators watched the first Final at Kennington Oval, having paid an admission fee of a shilling (5p)—a notable sum at that time. Year by year, support grew until it was necessary to move the Final to Crystal Palace where, by the end of the century, crowds of 100,000 and more were seeking admission, although not all of them could see the match from its grassy slopes.

Every Cup Final after the move until the war of 1914-18 was played at Crystal Palace, the largest crowd ever assembling there being that of 120,081, which saw Aston Villa defeat Sunderland by three goals to two in 1913, in what was probably one of the finest Finals ever played. Nor was this surprising, for both teams contained a number of internationals, and throughout the season they had been consistently at the top of the First Division. At the end of it, Sunderland won the championship by four points—a consolation for their narrow failure in the Final.

During the first world war, Crystal Palace was taken over as a depot by the armed forces, and the first post-war finals were therefore played on Chelsea's ground at Stamford Bridge. Then, in April 1923, Wembley staged its first Final, amongst some of the most amazing scenes ever to occur at a football match anywhere. At that time, security arrangements were far from adequate and only stand seats were reserved. A vast crowd overran the stadium, and when the two teams came out, the playing pitch was virtually invisible. By the exercise of immense skill the police, under the guidance of an inspector on a white horse, gradually moved the crowd back, although not as far as the touchline. Under these extraordinary conditions the game was played, Bolton Wanderers defeating West Ham United by two goals to none. By a miracle, no lives were lost, although there were many injuries, but this episode paved the way for the present all-ticket Finals. (Picture, p53.)

In the second year of the competition, in the 1872-3 season, the Wanderers were again the winners, their opponents being Oxford University, who had been beaten in the semi-final. Their appearance was due to the fact that their victorious opponents, Queen's Park, were unable to raise the fare. By 1874, the number of entries had risen to twenty-eight, and Sheffield had entered for the first time, reaching the semi-final, but throughout the 'seventies, the competition was still dominated by the Wanderers, the Royal Engineers, Oxford University, and the Old Etonians. Of these, only the Royal Engineers failed to win the Cup, although they appeared in several Finals. The Wanderers, in winning it three times in successive seasons, won the Cup outright, but immediately presented it back again to the Football Association.

The organisation of football was growing fast in the mid-seventies. Both Birmingham and Manchester formed associations, affiliated to the FA, but strong efforts to preserve a single association for the United Kingdom had failed. Scotland, Wales, and Ireland now had their national associations, and as a mark of their status, international games were being organised. By this date the problem of travelling costs had been eliminated, for the 'gates' could be relied on to cover expenses. The vast crowds which were soon to make it plain that Association football was the most popular national game were already taking shape. International matches, therefore, became a regular feature of the football season.

Throughout the 'seventies, there was a clear division between the football played in the south of England, and that played in the north and in Scotland. The great southern sides were composed principally of old public school or university men. They played robustly, early anticipating what came later to be described as the Corinthian style—none more enthusiastically than those early pioneers of the game, Alcock, Marindin and Lord Kinnaird. The north could not draw upon a similar reservoir of talent. The northern clubs, and those of Scotland, were drawn from the ranks of working-men, often miners. What they lacked in robustness, they made up for in skill, and there gradually seeped into the game the idea that special skill deserved reward. In the late 'seventies, there was a steady and increasing drift from Scotland to north-country clubs, and it was scarcely open to question that financial inducements, direct or indirect, brought them across the border. It was not long before the effects of this migration became apparent. In the course of a few seasons, the annual Cup competition came to be dominated by clubs whose professionalism was only thinly disguised. When Blackburn Olympic beat the Old Etonians in the Final in 1883, it marked the first step in the decline of the pure amateurism of the Old Boys' clubs. The new names which year by year were enrolled on the list of Cup-winners belonged to clubs from the north and midlands, who were recruiting from very far afield players who were certainly paid, even though this was not openly admitted.

The whole question came to a head in January 1884 when, after a drawn Cup-tie between Preston North End and Upton Park, the latter club protested that Preston had included players who were paid. Preston was therefore disqualified, but at the hearing before the Association, the Preston chairman, Major Sudell (a Preston millowner) admitted without qualification that his players were paid for time lost from their occupations, but he added that many clubs outside the ring of Old Boys' clubs and the Services were in a similar position. Following this episode, the Association could no longer avoid a decision, and under Alcock's leadership, it decided to admit professional players to clubs within its jurisdiction, but for some years afterwards it refrained from any effective measures of control. It was only after the formation of the League, and the growth of a transfer system as an alternative to the widespread poaching of leading players, that the Football Association was at length compelled to draw up its own rules governing the registration, payment and transfer of professional players. For some time after the historic decision on 'broken time' in 1884, the Association attempted to

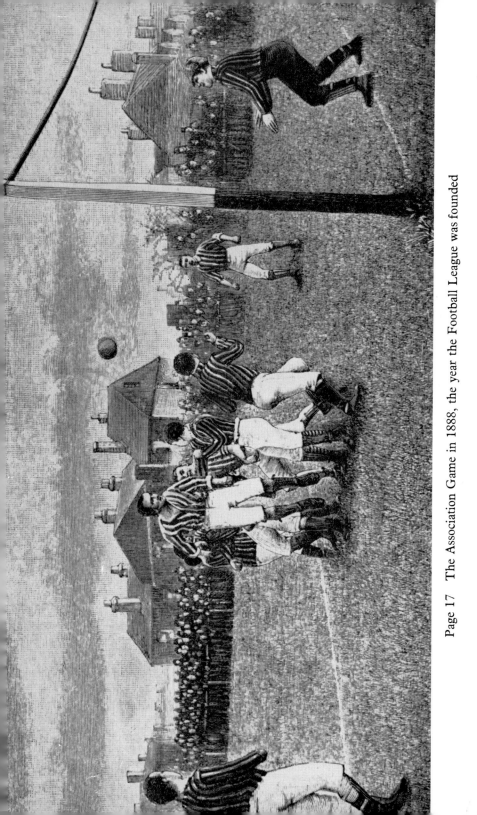

Page 17   The Association Game in 1888, the year the Football League was founded

Page 18 The Cup Final at Kennington Oval in 1891 : Blackburn Rovers *v* Notts County

ensure that clubs only paid money for lost wages on the basis of one day a week. But evasions were numerous, and the attempt was quickly abandoned.

Although the echoes of the struggle were a long time dying away, the decision of 1884 had far-reaching results. Suggested restrictions, including a proposal to bar professionals from Cup-matches, were abandoned. This proposed restriction had almost brought about the secession of the Lancashire clubs and the formation of an independent association. Fortunately, a split was avoided, and in 1885 the general meeting of the Football Association passed a code of rules relating to professionals which opened the way to a rapid development of professional football nationally and (within the United Kingdom) internationally. Professionals were to be allowed to play in all matches, including Cup-ties and internationals, subject to a qualification by birth, or two years' residence within six miles of the ground. They could not play for more than one club in a season without the permission of the Football Association, and they were ineligible to be members of the Association, or to serve on any of its committees, or to represent the club at any meeting of the Association. Finally, an annual registration with the Association was required before a professional was eligible to play.

The other national associations were slower to come into line with the FA, and some county associations remained for some time hostile to the introduction of professional players, but the battle was really over. Significantly, the same year was the last in which an amateur club—Queen's Park, from Glasgow—was ever to appear in the final of the English Cup. The eclipse of the amateur clubs in this competition paved the way for the introduction of the Amateur Cup Competition. For some time yet, nevertheless, outstanding amateur players were able to hold their own with, and even to beat, the best professional sides when playing for the famous Corinthians, who were at their peak in the middle years of the 'eighties. They might well have won the Cup more than once during this period, but for the fact that one of the terms of their foundation was that they should not enter this

B

competition—a rule which was only relaxed later, when the greatest days of the Corinthians were already past.

The midlands had been slower than Lancashire to go over to professionalism, but the successes of Blackburn Olympic, Blackburn Rovers, and Preston North End emphasised that success would now be governed by the quality of the professional players engaged, with the superior team work which ensued. In some matches between professionals and amateurs, the amateurs were not only defeated, but completely outclassed. At the same time, the engagement of professional players, even at the extremely modest wages which were offered, gave rise to the demand for regular Saturday fixtures over a wider area than these had hitherto been generally made. Football was booming, and the introduction of the compulsory half-holiday, which for the manual worker was normally Saturday afternoon, held the promise that crowds would continue to grow. This resulted in the formation of the Football League in 1888, to be followed shortly afterwards by the formation of other leagues, of which the most important were the Southern and Midland Leagues, in which professional clubs could be assured of a regular fixture list. The original twelve founder-members of the Football League (in the order in which they finished the first season) were: Preston North End, Aston Villa, Wolverhampton Wanderers, Blackburn Rovers, Bolton Wanderers, West Bromwich Albion, Accrington, Everton, Burnley, Derby County, Notts County and Stoke. In that season, Preston North End had achieved a distinction which is not likely to be repeated. They won the League Championship without losing a match, and they won the Cup without having a goal scored against them.

In the eighty years which have elapsed since the Football League was formed, the fortunes of the original twelve members have fluctuated greatly. Preston North End, Aston Villa, Wolverhampton Wanderers, Blackburn Rovers, Bolton Wanderers and West Bromwich Albion all won a principal share of League and Cup honours, with the rest (except Accrington) appearing from time to time. As the League has extended, and competition has become keener, every one of these clubs in turn descended to the Second Division, and more recently Preston North End, Aston Villa, Wolverhampton Wanderers, Stoke, Blackburn Rovers and Bolton Wanderers have suffered the indignity of descending to the Third. For too long in the period since 1945, Notts County have lived precariously in the Fourth Division, but at long last, in 1970-71, they won promotion to the Third by a margin which suggests that their revival will take them still higher. Accrington, after descending by stages to the Fourth, ultimately became one of the very few clubs to find the financial commitments of modern football too much for them, and they were compelled to withdraw in 1962, to make way for Oxford United, a club whose success has been conspicuous in the same period.

The attraction of League football is quite distinct from that of the Cup competition, which year to year induces sports writers to use such terms as 'glamour', 'drama', and 'magic' to describe its appeal. The appeal of a competition in which the results of a single game can decide a club's fortunes for the season is very great, and particularly because it can produce pairings which bring small and relatively unknown clubs temporarily into prominence. Since 1945, at various times Yeovil, Colchester United and Oxford United (the two last not then League clubs) have provided sensations by beating a succession of strong opponents from the Football League. In the 1970-71 season, Colchester United, now a member of the Fourth Division, revived memories of their earlier exploits by decisively beating Leeds United 3—2 at Colchester. Such victories, owing much to enthusiasm, not only of players but of supporters, may not only bring a handsome immediate financial reward, but rekindle local pride in the club. This can happen at an even higher level. In 1920, Huddersfield Town were a struggling Second Division club, which was on the point of moving to Leeds because of tepid support. Unexpectedly, they fought their way to the Cup Final, and the enthusiasm generated on the way was sufficient to win them promotion to the First Division. The result was one of the League's major success stories. Under the direction of one of the greatest football managers, Herbert Chapman, they won the Cup once, won promotion, and the League three times in successive seasons between 1920 and 1930. In between, they appeared in three other Cup Finals, and twice finished second in the First Division. In one of these seasons, when they were again chasing the elusive 'double' of League and Cup, after a strenuous Cup-tie they visited Burnley in the League, and played one regular first-team player—the goalkeeper. They were fined £250 by the League for fielding a *weak* team; but it had, in fact, won 3—1. Those years of greatness have placed Huddersfield Town among the really great clubs of football. They also made their early struggles no more than a distant memory.

When the Football League was formed, a number of well-known northern and midland clubs had been left outside its membership. These, after a brief independent existence, became the Second Division in 1892. The original twelve members had already been increased to fourteen in 1891 and again to sixteen in 1892. This had brought in famous clubs such as Manchester United, Sheffield Wednesday and Nottingham Forest. The new Second Division was more experimental. It comprised originally: Ardwick (which later became Manchester City), Birmingham (now Birmingham City), Bootle, Burton United, Crewe Alexandra, Darwen, Grimsby Town, Lincoln City, Northwich Victoria, Port Vale, Sheffield United and Walsall Town Swifts. These names will show how rapidly professional football had spread in the midlands, and although not all of these clubs preserved their League status—notably, Bootle, Burton United, Darwen and Walsall Swifts—the enthusiasm for football in these areas was very great, and all of them for a time enjoyed considerable success. In the end, like Accrington much later, they were defeated only by increasing competition for support; and finally, although Walsall Swifts are no more, their present-day successors, Walsall, have a secure position in the League and once defeated Arsenal in a Cup-tie.

The League clubs have had the most varied, and sometimes unexpected, beginnings, but before mentioning some of them, something must be said about the growth of the Football League itself. It is sometimes attacked for undue conservatism, but whilst for the most part it prefers to proceed cautiously, there have been occasions when really bold innovations have been made. By stages the League was extended until, in 1919, there were two divisions each comprising twenty-two clubs. Its area had extended to include the three northern clubs—Newcastle United, Sunderland (a great and successful side in the first fourteen years of the century) and Middlesbrough, together with the first of the London clubs, Arsenal, Tottenham Hotspur, Chelsea, Fulham, Clapton Orient and West Ham United. Then, in the season 1920-21, a Third Division of twenty-two clubs was added, mainly recruited from the Southern League, which was no longer the powerful rival it had been at the beginning of the century when Tottenham and Southampton had appeared in Cup Finals, and Tottenham had even broken the Football League's monopoly of that trophy. In this way, some very notable southern clubs joined the Football League, having some time before ended their efforts to remain amateur. To mention only a few, they included Luton Town, Millwall, Norwich City, Portsmouth, Brentford, Crystal Palace, Swindon Town, Plymouth Argyle and Swansea. This southern Third Division was balanced in the following season by a northern section, thereby enabling some of the lesser clubs, such as Accrington Stanley, Crewe Alexandra, Lincoln City and Walsall, who had played parts in the early history of the League, to return to League football. The last step in the expansion of the League was taken in 1951 when the number of clubs in each of the Third Divisions was increased to twenty-four. Finally, in 1958, the Third Division was divided on achievement into Third and Fourth Divisions on a national basis.

In 1960-61, the Football League introduced a League Cup (as the Scottish Football League had done some time before). In eleven years it has established itself firmly as a national competition with a character of its own, as may be realised from the fact that two clubs then in the Third Division have won the trophy, in each case defeating First Division opponents. Possibly one reason for this is that, whilst in the 'English' Cup the First and Second Division clubs are exempted until the third rounds, by which time a considerable number of Third and Fourth Division clubs are eliminated, in the League Cup all clubs enter together and the casualty rate amongst the members of the two upper divisions in the early rounds can be (and has been) high.

A question which is often discussed in the daily press is the policy of the League in respect of its membership. In the First and Second Divisions, the two bottom clubs are automatically relegated, and the two clubs finishing highest in the Second and Third Divisions are automatically promoted. From the Fourth Division, four clubs are promoted, in place of four Third Division clubs, which are relegated. At the bottom of the Fourth Division, four clubs retire but may be re-elected. Whilst, therefore, the composition of the First Division changes annually by two clubs only, that of the Second Division includes four new members, and that of the Third Division changes by the exchange of six clubs. It is no accident, therefore, that the institution of a national Third Division has been a conspicuous success. The quality of the football played has improved, and gates have tended to increase steadily, especially when historic clubs have been relegated to it.

Even under the present system, clubs can decline with remarkable rapidity. At various times, Grimsby, Oldham Athletic, Notts County and Brentford and, more recently, Luton Town and Northampton Town have descended abruptly from the First to the Fourth Division. Luton's return to the Second Division was nearly as rapid as the club's descent. On the other hand, Crystal Palace and Ipswich have climbed from the Fourth to the First. It need scarcely be stated what serious problems face directors and managers when a club descends to the lower regions of the League. Support dwindles, players are reluctant to play for a losing club, and finance becomes very scarce. Even success has its penalties. Players expect to earn more, transfer fees are higher, and increased support may not compensate for the heavier expenditure. One can therefore understand the reluctance of clubs to favour a bolder policy, involving an increase in the numbers of those relegated and promoted.

It is possibly the other end of the League that incurs the heaviest criticism—when, for example, a club in the Fourth Division is reported to be in serious difficulties. Yet the surprising thing is that these difficulties practically never result in a voluntary withdrawal. Civic pride is usually too deeply involved for the League status to be lost, for when it is, the club reverts to some less attractive competition which rarely receives the attention of sports writers, and very frequently the club's finances only permit the engagement of part-time players. It is sometimes argued, nevertheless, that a bolder policy should be followed in the election of new clubs in place of Fourth Division members who have been unsuccessful over a number of years, and in support of it, it can be argued that Oxford United, Cambridge United, Shrewsbury Town, Peterborough United, Scunthorpe United, Colchester United, and Workington Town—all elected in the post-war period—have established their places. Moreover, at each annual general meeting of the League there is always a substantial number of applications, almost invariably from clubs which have recently been enjoying considerable playing success in their leagues, and also in the earlier rounds of the competition for the English Cup. One criticism which may perhaps be made is that it is in the Fourth Division that travelling is the heaviest burden. It involves journeys from Exeter and Torquay to Workington, Grimsby, Darlington and Hartlepools. In any future schemes of expansion, a new grouping of clubs into a Fourth (North) and a Fourth (South), possibly with a reduction in the number of clubs in those two divisions, and also in the Third, to twenty-two or even to twenty, might well be considered. It would ease the heavy burden on clubs which have great difficulty in controlling expenses, whilst satisfying the ambitions of numerous clubs on the fringes of the League. If, in addition, it were provided that three clubs from each section of a reconstituted Fourth Division were promoted to the Third

Division, from which therefore six clubs were relegated annually, greater movement at the lower end of the League ladder would have been secured.

The world of football—and particularly of professional football—is never static. When English football appeared to have become stereotyped, shock defeats from leading continental sides in both international and club matches rejuvenated it, and the introduction of a number of European cup competitions and, above all, of the World Cup competition, have ensured that methods of play should be constantly subjected to the most searching criticism. Equally, football is no respecter of great names, and if a club with an illustrious past (and none have a more distinguished past record than Aston Villa and Preston North End) fails to move with the times, it will not be able to escape relegation, with all its attendant problems. There is, after all, no magic in a great name. Nevertheless, it may be valuable to recall, briefly, some of the vicissitudes of several of the more famous League clubs, and to mention some of their greatest triumphs.

The early dominance of Preston North End and Aston Villa have already been noticed. In those early years, Preston owed almost everything to the vision and courage of their chairman, Major Sudall, who led the battle to legalise professionalism. Aston Villa grew out of the Sunday-school boys of a Wesleyan chapel, who from 1874 onwards played in a rough field near Perry Bar. Under the skilful guidance of a Glasgow Scot named George Ramsay, they formed themselves into a regular club, skilfully coached by him, and hired a ground for the sum of £5 a year. Their spectacular upward climb to six League Championships, and six successful campaigns for the FA Cup, was firmly launched in the early 'eighties, culminating in 1897 (the year that they moved to Villa Park) with winning both League and Cup, thus equalling Preston North End's achievement. These two double triumphs remained unmatched, in spite of the efforts of outstanding teams such as Huddersfield Town and the Arsenal in the inter-war period, until quite recently first Tottenham Hotspur, and then in 1970-71 the Arsenal, proved that the stresses of a long season were not too great for the 'double' to be achieved again.

Over eighty years, League football has seen a succession of great clubs achieve a temporary pre-eminence over their rivals. Close behind their Midland rivals came West Bromwich Albion and Wolverhampton Wanderers, each with notable triumphs in League and Cup. Possibly the greatest achievements of Wolverhampton Wanderers were during the managerships of Major Buckley and Stanley Cullis, when, led by England's captain, Wright (who gained over 100 international caps), the club pioneered the entry of English clubs into European football, whilst both the League Championship and the Cup were won.

The history of the major League clubs is a chapter of modern English social history which deserves more attention than it has yet received. To many, they are regarded as a symbol of municipal achievement, with which ordinary people are in some way closely connected. This close association finds its clearest expression when the club wins some much-contested trophy. Custom now decrees that on such occasions the victorious team, carrying the trophy, should ride through the town on the top of a bus, amid wildly-cheering crowds, to the town hall, where a reception from the mayor and leading citizens awaits them. Such demonstrations may no longer greet the return of a popular member to the House of Commons, but each season in the football world they seem to grow in size and fervour.

Possibly these demonstrations are a tribute to the resolution of those who have brought the successful club to its present eminence. Although in more recent times clubs have sometimes been deliberately created—as Chelsea were created in 1905—with the intention that they should reach the pinnacle of achievement in the shortest space of time, most clubs have had to struggle for existence in their early years. This is remarkably illustrated by the history of Tottenham Hotspur (one of the most colourfully-named of all football clubs). Founded in 1882 to give Tottenham boys who played cricket in summer a winter game, they limped along with no money and no settled headquarters. Sometimes, it is recorded, the committee met in the street by a lamp-post, where, by the light of the gas jet, the secretary was able to read the minutes and record decisions. For some years, the club played on Tottenham Marshes, but they later relinquished this and moved to Northumberland Park to an enclosed ground. Like most southern clubs, they clung stubbornly to their amateur status until, in 1893, they were fined by the London FA and their ground was closed for a fortnight as a penalty for buying one of their players, who had joined them from Fulham, a pair of boots for 10s (50p). The episode attracted attention, and support grew considerably. In 1895, Tottenham became a professional club and joined the Southern League, winning the championship in 1900. A year later they defeated Sheffield United, at that time probably the greatest cup-fighting team in the country, in a replay at Bolton after a drawn game at Crystal Palace before a crowd of over 110,000. Tottenham thus became the only Southern League club, or for that matter the only club not a member of the Football League, after its foundation, to win the Cup. Their success paved the way for their entry into the Second Division of the Football League in 1909, winning promotion to the First Division in their first season.

The history of Tottenham's greatest rivals, the Arsenal, is also one of many changes of fortune, with periods when the future of this great club was really uncertain. Their name, possibly the best known of all English clubs, may seem surprising to modern supporters. It recalls that the club was founded, in 1886, by employees of Woolwich Arsenal, from workers in the Dial Square workshops, and its first name was the Dial Square AFC. Until the end of the century, still an amateur club, they did not survive the qualifying rounds of the Cup competition and were unsuccessful in 1892 in their efforts to persuade other southern clubs to form what became, a couple of years later, the Southern League. By this time, however, Woolwich Arsenal (as they had now become) had turned professional, and had joined the Second Division of the Football League, where they remained until the end of the 1904-5 season. By now, they had moved to Plumstead, and the connection with the Arsenal was at an end. Unfortunately, the situation of the ground was not a good one, so far as support was concerned, and Woolwich Arsenal remained a poor relation of the more popular First Division clubs until Henry Norris, who had been chairman of Fulham, moved to the Arsenal, and firmly directed the rise to greatness which followed. First, he engineered the audacious transfer of the club from Plumstead to Highbury, Woolwich being dropped from the club's name in the process. Secondly, he induced Herbert Chapman to move from his brilliantly successful managership at Huddersfield to Highbury in 1925. There followed years of sensational transfers and of staggering success, the memory of which remains even today. In 1927, the club reached the Final for the first time, only to lose to Cardiff City. They were back again in 1930, to beat Huddersfield Town—a game which Chapman must have watched with mixed feelings—and again in 1936 (two years after Chapman's death) to beat Sheffield United. In between, the League Championship had been won (in 1930-31), by what was then the record number of 66 points, and between 1932 and 1935, they emulated Huddersfield Town's great record by winning the League Championship in three successive seasons. The years of success also brought a complete transformation of the ground which, in the first years following the move from Plumstead, had boasted little more than an old iron stand. All this was changed, and the two present double-decker stands were built. Together with the excellent terracing at each end of the ground, they have transformed the Highbury headquarters into one of the most architecturally-satisfying grounds in the country. Even though the years which followed the war of 1939-45 brought few successes, something of the old tradition still remained. When, in 1970-71, Arsenal took a giant step on the road back by winning the League Championship as well as the FA Cup, many people besides Londoners felt that a national institution was at long last returning to its former splendour.

One further memory from the great years of the decade from

1925 to 1935 may be recalled. At that period, long before the idea of a team manager for the selection and training of an English international squad of players had been born, the selectors had gradually adopted the policy of building a side around the key players of the most successful club of the moment. Thus, after 1922 there had been a period when the players, first of Liverpool, and then of Huddersfield Town had dominated the English side, although selections from Huddersfield were limited by the fact that one or two of their greatest players, and notably that great winger Alex Jackson, were Scots. Just before the rise of the Arsenal, Sheffield Wednesday, then enjoying a spell of conspicuous success, habitually supplied five players to England's side. These included Blenkinsopp at back, and the entire half-back line. As the Wednesday side passed its peak, it was replaced by the Arsenal which, in one season, supplied no less than seven players.

Sheffield Wednesday is, of course, one of the two Sheffield clubs, each of which has enjoyed spells of greatness. Neither, as has been noticed, was a founder-member of the Football League, although Sheffield was one of the original homes of Association football, and the Sheffield club (always an amateur club) was for many years the oldest surviving club in the country, having been founded in 1855. Sheffield Wednesday was founded in 1867, originally (like Tottenham) as a cricket club, with football added to keep the club together in the winter. Fixtures were arranged for Wednesdays—hence the name. But cricket was soon dropped, and in 1886 the club decided to turn professional, thus marking the first stage in Sheffield's retreat from its obstinate adherence to the amateur game. Joining the League in 1891, the next fifteen years were years of constant success. The Cup was won three times, and the League twice.

Close behind them came Sheffield United which, like the Wednesday, was founded both for cricket and football—and both sports are maintained today. Founded in 1889, they followed their local rivals into the League, but in the Second Division, in 1892; and in the next few years they came close to equalling the record of their neighbours. The club earned promotion in its first season; it won the League Championship in 1898; it appeared in the Cup Finals of 1899, 1901, 1902, 1915 and 1925, and again in 1936, losing only in 1901 (to Tottenham) and in 1936 (to the Arsenal). In this period the club sometimes fielded ten internationals and regularly finished in one of the top places in the League.

The reasons for the striking successes of both Sheffield clubs at this period are not difficult to discover. Both responded to the promptings of a remarkable trio which included the brothers Clegg, both of whom were in their youth well-known athletes and soccer players of international quality. The elder, later Sir Charles, was for many years chairman of the Football Association, and his tenure of office overlapped the greatest periods in the history of the two clubs. Sir Charles was a good deal of an autocrat, in the clubs and in the Football Association, and his activities as president earned him fame (and caricature) in a series of articles in *Punch*, where he is described as 'The Emperor Clegg'. Yet football as a whole owes very much to his forthright direction. His brother, Sir William, though less colourful, was as shrewd, and in due course became lord mayor of Sheffield. The third member of the trio, again a distinguished footballer in his youth, was Arthur Dickenson, for many years a member of the FA Council and of the management committee of the Football League, where his influence was considerable.

The story of the two Sheffield clubs—which might be paralleled from a number of other leading cities, including Liverpool, Manchester, Huddersfield, Nottingham, and Hull—shows yet again the combination that is necessary to bring a club to greatness: an energetic and courageous directorate (or perhaps only a chairman, where his position is outstanding), a manager in whom the board reposes full confidence, and finally a group of players of high ability whom the manager has himself selected and trained. No one element alone is sufficient. Together they have in the past produced outstanding success.

2

The Modern Footballer

In the rapidly-changing society of modern Britain, no occupation has changed more profoundly than that of the professional footballer. The names of outstanding players have always been known nationally, but in the past that knowledge has been largely confined to followers of football. In their day, cricketers such as Jack Hobbs and Frank Woolley—to say nothing of Sir Donald Bradman—were known to wider sections of the public, both here and in Commonwealth countries, than Hapgood and Bastin of the Arsenal, or any other outstanding professional footballer of the inter-war years. With only very rare exceptions, their fame was temporary and local. It is very different today. Support for cricket has dwindled almost to vanishing point, and few could name more than one or two members of the last touring side to England (even if they knew from which Commonwealth country it came) or the members of the last English touring side to go abroad. On the other hand, the outstanding footballers of today are known nationally, and even internationally. The names of George Best, Bobby Moore, Pele and Eusebio are familiar in every country where football is played; and that is practically everywhere. Their exploits are followed with admiration, their photographs appear in newspapers and advertisements, and their lives are lived in a glare of publicity equalled only by that which envelops leading television stars, whose careers their own in some ways resemble. Like the television stars, they can be the idols of the public one day, and forgotten the next. Again, the rewards for these popular favourites can be very great, but they can end as abruptly if permanent injury or loss of form ends their playing careers.

There have been other, and more subtle changes. Until the

post-war years, watching professional football was considered to be the monopoly of the cloth-cap-and-scarf brigade. Today, university professors, authors and politicians make a parade of their support for famous League clubs, and Cabinet ministers find it good publicity to be seen in earnest conversation with some outstanding player. The image of the professional footballer has changed completely. He is no longer regarded simply as an employee. His views, not only on football, are given the widest publicity; so are his reactions to the game. For some of the players with the greatest following, journalism can be a lucrative second string, even though, upon occasion, their views may involve them in conflict with club or league. Even so, the footballer hauled before a disciplinary committee for writing disrespectfully about those who control his career can afford to look on its activities with a certain amount of detachment—or at any rate with greater detachment than his predecessor in the pre-war world. Any fine will be trifling in comparison with his income, and too much money has been expended upon his acquisition and training for anything more than a short suspension to be contemplated. And even a short suspension may be a blessing in disguise. It may give the player a rest from the tension of recurrent matches, and since he probably has business commitments as well, he may have temporarily rather more time in which to attend to them. Again like television stars, the successful footballer of today may be involved in a wide variety of business—from hat shops and boutiques to sports gear and restaurants—and he may give employment to many different people, from accountants to door-to-door salesmen. As yet there is no certainty that playing football has produced its first British millionaire, but this has certainly happened abroad. In the meantime, expensive cars, country houses and lavish living, including patronage of expensive nightclubs, have become the hall-mark of success in the game in England, even though recognition in a nightclub on the wrong night may lead to some hard talking, and perhaps disciplinary action, during the rigorous training of the playing season.

This is by no means all. Footballers have now attained the dizzy heights of the Honours List. The incomparable services of Matt Busby to Manchester United, and less directly, to the game as a whole; the success of Alf Ramsay in steering England to victory in the World Cup in 1966; and the record-breaking playing career of Stanley Matthews, terminating only when he had passed his fiftieth birthday, have all been rewarded with knighthoods, and there have been lesser honours for other players. Significantly, in the period during which these distinctions have been earned by these men, all of whom in their day were outstanding professional footballers, the only administrator or club director to be similarly honoured was the late Joseph Richards, who was for a number of years president of the Football League. Clearly, there has been a shift of emphasis. Today, the spotlight is always upon the player. To ever more substantial financial rewards, there is now added the possibility of public honours. It is perhaps not too fanciful to conjecture that in the near future we may see some national footballing idol elevated to the House of Lords. If England were Brazil, and if Bobby Moore were Pele, he might already be there.

What has been responsible for this astonishing change in the position of the professional footballer, and in the public attitude towards him? Until the end of the last war, the ordinary footballer was not regarded as being very different from a skilled employee of a firm. There was a fixed maximum wage for his services, and it is somewhat startling to remember that, until 1939, this was no more than four pounds a week, to which there could be added a bonus of two pounds for a win, and a pound for a draw. All indirect payments, whether in cash or kind, were heavily penalised, and the decisions of controlling bodies upon infractions passed unchallenged, and normally without comment. In the prevailing climate, it was for the employers to dictate the terms upon which the game was played, and it was also for the employers to say how long they wished to retain a player's services. Again, there was no comprehensive provision for a player when his services were at an end. It is true that there were few

Page 35   The Cup Final of 1902, when Sheffield United drew with
Southampton

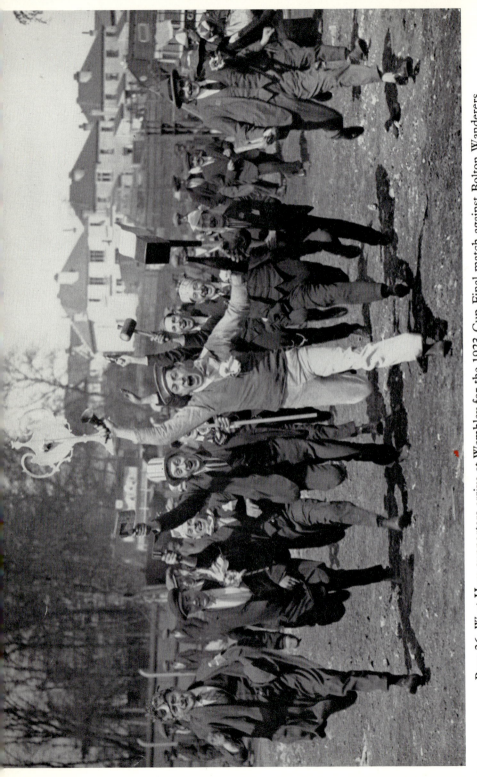

Page 36 West Ham supporters arrive at Wembley for the 1923 Cup Final match against Bolton Wanderers

pension funds for industrial employees either; but the playing career of the professional footballer was brief. Under the most favourable conditions, it would usually end in the late thirties. Thereafter, a small 'sweets-and-tobacco' shop, or the managership of a public house (often in the vicinity of the ground on which he had played) was the best the ordinary player could anticipate. For others, there might be casual, and possibly intermittent employment as a scout for a club, or even part-time employment on the ground, but the rewards were pitifully small. For the fortunate few, there might be managerships of other professional clubs. Even in those days, tenure of such a post was often conditioned by playing success, although the casualty rate among managers was much less than it is today. Even with these limitations, the career of a professional footballer was not unattractive, and a few of the most gifted might hope to combine it with a career in first-class cricket. Outstanding among such were the Compton brothers and Joe Hulme (all three internationals in both cricket and football) and, in an earlier era, Hardinge and Ashdown, two colourful Kent batsmen, the brothers Gunn of Nottinghamshire, Hendren of Middlesex, J. T. Sharp and Harry Makepeace of Everton and Lancashire, and above all the incomparable C. B. Fry.

It is highly unlikely that anyone will win international honours in both cricket and football again. So far as cricket is concerned, there are now so many tours that it would be impossible to consider a footballer seriously for inclusion, because of the inroads which it would make upon his professional career. Moreover, the football season is now longer than it used to be, so that conflict between the two sports would be greater. More importantly, however, football is now a whole-time career (which, at the top, also includes a number of foreign tours) with only a brief summer vacation, which is largely confined to July. Even so, summer tours have now extended to July. If there were to be the possibility of competition, the very much greater rewards of football would decisively tip the scales.

In the course of two decades, the entire pattern of professional

C

football, at Football League level, has been transformed, and the casual approach of an earlier age has been abandoned. In the early post-war years this at first seemed good enough to preserve the traditional English supremacy over continental rivals. In spite of occasional shocks, this conviction survived until the historic encounter between Hungary and England at Wembley in 1953. In that game it was not so much that the Hungarians proved the winners by the comfortable margin of 6—3, but that they outclassed a good English side in all departments of the game, revealing a fluidity of movement and a directness of attack which left their opponents struggling in pursuit. From that day onwards, England (and also Scotland, Wales and Ireland) struggled with new conceptions of the game, in which intricate patterns were woven, and in which the century-old design of two backs, three half-backs and five forwards disappeared into history. Even the conventional names of players disappeared. To-day, we no longer have backs, half-backs and forwards, but defenders, strikers and linkmen. Moves and counter-moves are plotted with the care and intricacy of gambits in chess, and there are prolonged discussions upon the effectiveness of rival formations, whether 4—2—4, 4—3—3, or any other possible combination. What is at once apparent, even to the uninstructed spectator, is that football is now a game (or perhaps an encounter) in which skill, power and brains are combined, and that the modern footballer is an accomplished athlete, who must make the most strenuous efforts to remain at the peak of physical fitness during a long and extremely exhausting playing season. As a not unnatural result, the playing life of the top-class player is tending to become shorter. Sir Stanley Matthews continued to play first-class football until he was turned fifty, and he even made occasional appearances afterwards. Billy Meredith turned out for Manchester City in a Cup-tie in the late 'twenties, at the age of fifty-one. But it is most unlikely that any player of today will last so long. Like the boxer and the professional tennis star, he must reach the top early, and look forward to approximately fifteen to seventeen years in the highest class of football.

At the top, the game today is faster and more accurate than it has ever been, and games are planned as collective efforts, shaped towards the known weaknesses of particular opponents. Whereas in the past a forward might expect to be in a scoring position on quite a number of occasions during a match, opportunities today are few, and a striker's ability is measured in part by his ability to turn even a half-chance to account. Nothing less than ninety minutes' all-out effort, both physical and mental, is needed. Accordingly, the modern footballer differs from his predecessors in being swifter both in thought and execution. He is trained to a greater degree of alertness, and it is no accident that among the household names of modern professional football there are found to be university graduates, accountants and members of other professions.

Football abounds with stories of unknown youths who have walked into some of the country's most famous grounds, have asked for a trial, and have subsequently won international honours. Such incidents happen occasionally today. For example, Stephen Heighway (a graduate) played for Skelmersdale in the Amateur Cup Final at the close of one season, won a regular place in Liverpool's talented side in the next, and appeared (unhappily on the losing side) again at Wembley in the FA Cup Final at the close of the next. This is one of the episodes which give colour to modern football, but they are rare, and are becoming rarer. Today, the stars of the future are picked out whilst still at school, possibly playing in schoolboy international matches; they are signed on apprenticeship forms as soon as they are old enough, and are carefully trained and drafted into youth elevens, for which national competitions are organised. Many others pass through training sessions, and sometimes through junior elevens, in most clubs, but only a few are retained. Naturally, when the rewards of the successful player are so very high, competition becomes steadily keener, and the searches undertaken by clubs become more comprehensive. On the other hand, the investment which a club makes in training at all stages is now so comprehensive that it cannot afford to make many mistakes in selection. To this is linked the anxiety that a promising young novice may be allowed to slip out of the club's hands, into those of a rival. Before he signs professional forms the young player has an unrestricted choice of clubs, and many factors will influence his decision. These may include local attachments, the glamour which is inseparable from playing for a fashionable club, welfare schemes, and training for a career when his playing days end; but in the last resort it will now be the financial prospects which influence him most. The discrepancy between the rewards available for playing in the First Division, in contrast with playing in a lower one, the possibility of lucrative Cup runs, and above all of playing games in Europe or even further afield, will play a considerable part in making the final decision. Moreover, a young player knows that his skill is likely to develop more fully when playing football with the outstanding players of the day, and also that he is likely to receive more publicity from press, television and other news media in such company, than he will in less glamorous surroundings. Football is not a career in which success comes in predictable stages. An injury to an established player may find a replacement suddenly appearing in the first team whilst he is still in his teens. Every established player knows that some youngster is ready and eager to replace him. In this respect, his career is even more competitive than that of a popular entertainer.

These developments have, in turn, produced important and far-reaching changes in the management of clubs. When players' wages were standardised and low in comparison with present-day rewards, it was not unusual for a club to have a playing strength of thirty to forty professionals. Some might be long past their best, but if they had served the club well their retention was not a great commitment, and there was the possibility that they might be useful in an emergency. Further, some clubs for a time ran a number of sides, in addition to a regular reserve side. If the rules of the leagues in which these junior sides played permitted it, one or two older professionals might be included to coach and encourage the youngsters. In the 'fifties, one or two

First Division clubs regularly put out between six and ten sides each week. Today all this is changed. A number of professional clubs now function with only sixteen, eighteen or twenty professionals, and a player whose direct utility has ended is not retained. In any case the services which he might have given in training junior sides are no longer needed. Training today is as professional as actual playing. It is in the hands of specialists and, in any case, the number of junior sides has been reduced or they may have been abolished altogether. The future success of the club is now centred upon the youth side, whose performances are very closely followed. Success in the national competition may be a pointer to the club's training policy.

Some time in the early 'sixties Association football played by the League clubs, especially in the first two divisions of the Football League, became big business without ceasing to be a game. In retrospect, the change was inevitable, and it was principally the result of two factors. The first was the entry of clubs into European competitions, which could not only be very profitable in themselves but could also stimulate interest in the club at home, with a consequent rise in gate receipts. The second was the abolition of any upper limit on players' wages. From this point onwards, players have become entertainers as well as athletes and their performances are judged by new standards. Further, although football crowds have only in rare instances increased in recent years (and even then, only whilst the club has been successful), there has been an inescapable increase in admission charges, more especially for seating and covered accommodation, so that the gate receipts of the successful club are now very high. For example, whereas the receipts for the Cup Final used to be in the neighbourhood of £20,000, in 1971 they exceeded £120,000. Even taking into account the decline in the value of money, these receipts are still high. Of course, the picture at the other end of the Football League is a very different one. Here, unfashionable clubs struggle along without any but the most local publicity, always in debt and sometimes on the brink of dissolution. Players' wages are still modest. Some of them may be part-timers, and the club could not continue to exist without frequent donations from supporters' clubs. Attendances at Fourth Division games towards the end of a season make melancholy reading. Two or three thousand only may be present. Even so, there is never any lack of applicants for entry to the League, and very few clubs have retired voluntarily at any period of the League's history. Every aspirant to League status believes it can make a success of League football, and the striking rise of Oxford United to the Second Division is an example of what may be done by persistence and unremitting effort.

There is yet another side to the story. Luton Town and Northampton Town at times seemed to occupy a safe place in the First Division. Both fell rapidly to the Fourth, from which Luton, by shrewd management, returned to the Second. Two clubs with a distinguished history—both at one time members of the First Division, and both Cup winners—Nottingham County and Oldham Athletic, lingered for many years, virtually forgotten, in the Fourth Division, playing before a handful of supporters. The success of both in gaining promotion to the Third Division in the 1970-71 season marks the revival of two clubs which seemed to be beyond it. Still more spectacular, perhaps, was the decline of Aston Villa and Preston North End, two clubs which have won every honour that English football offers, and whose early history had much to do with the establishment of Association football in its prominent place in the national life. 'Proud Preston' returned to the Second Division at the end of the season 1970-71, and Aston Villa missed promotion in the same season by only a narrow margin, but for both clubs the road back has not been an easy one. Finally, at the end of the 1970-71 season, the fall of Blackpool and Burnley to the Second Division, and of Bolton and Blackburn (both among the greatest clubs of an earlier era) to the Third must be a matter of concern to all Lancastrians proud of the great part their clubs have played in the development of the game.

Frequently, the vicissitudes of a professional football club may be traced to circumstances entirely beyond its control. Of these, the foremost is trade depression and local unemployment. At the end of the first war, Cardiff City were for a time the outstanding club in England and Wales. Their decline in the 'thirties coincided, not only with the national depression of those years, but also with the progressive disappearance of Cardiff's coal trade and great distress in the Welsh coalfields. Sunderland's present lowly position in the Second Division, which stands in sharp contrast to its great achievements in the two decades before 1914, is closely linked with the present exceptionally high unemployment in that area. The truth is that falling gates exercise a depressive influence far beyond the actual fall in numbers. It is as if a general lethargy descends. Moreover, players themselves may be reluctant to come to such an area, and may feel dispirited if they already live in it.

It is possible to trace this connection between a club's success or failure and the prosperity or decline of the town in which it operates a good deal further, and that success or failure may also be affected by the success or failure of other clubs in that area. The long decline in the fortunes of Nottingham County (now happily over) was underlined by the success of their local rivals, Nottingham Forest. The decline of a whole collection of Lancashire clubs has been partly due to the continued success of the two Liverpool clubs, Liverpool and Everton, and the two Manchester clubs. Today, motor-cars make short work of distance and an enthusiastic supporter will think nothing of travelling forty or fifty miles to see his club play. On the fringes of most of our big cities are clubs struggling hard to keep afloat. They include Tranmere Rovers, competing with the Liverpool clubs; Rotherham, competing with the Sheffield clubs; Halifax and York, competing with Leeds United, and Huddersfield Town; and Walsall, on the doorstep of the Birmingham clubs.

These have survived, but a number have not. Accrington Stanley (one of the original twelve clubs which formed the

Football League), Aberdare Athletic, Gateshead, Bradford Park Avenue, New Brighton, Ashington, Nelson, Wigan Borough and some others have all fallen from League status, primarily because of industrial decline and competition from successful clubs.

Those who are responsible for the success or failure of a League club must take these factors into account, and also some others. A board of directors may be willing to spend, but a credit squeeze may have dried up credit. A manager may know precisely the player he needs to bring success to his efforts, but he may not be able to persuade a club to part with him, or even if the club is willing, he may not be able to persuade the player to come. There are also a number of imponderables which affect decisions. A player on the way up is usually unwilling to join a club in a lower division, and a player, not unnaturally, often regards himself as on the way up longer than does his club. Again, a player may already have a second source of income in a business which he is unwilling to leave, or his wife may not like the north, or the south, as the case may be; she may protest at the thought of leaving her friends, or she herself may have a job which she does not wish to give up. Even if all these difficulties are smoothed away, another club may appear on the scene with a better offer. Since a player receives 10 per cent of the transfer fee, if he is being transferred at the request of his club, this is a matter of financial interest to him.

Sufficient indication has been given of the complexities of modern football management. It is therefore not surprising that this has changed to a degree at least equal to the change in the players' status. It is not without significance that it is the manager, and not the board, which is now the centre of interest and activity, or that of the first three footballers to receive knighthoods, two were successful managers. Before 1914, the boards of directors of many professional football clubs contained a substantial number of men who themselves had been amateur footballers of high distinction. For many years, a high-level knowledge of football was regarded as a prerequisite for election to the board. That generation of football administrators has now passed. Their successors are mainly business-men who are elected for their ability to introduce money to the club, and who are seeking a congenial environment in which to undertake some public service in the town or area where they live or carry on business. Their introduction has been followed by important changes. They have frequently looked with dismay at the make-shift administrations with which many clubs have lived in the past, and they have introduced administrative systems which bear some resemblance to the systems which exist in the world of industry and commerce. Similarly, they have for the most part dissociated themselves from the day-to-day running of the club. They have regarded the officials they have appointed as accountable to the board, but otherwise free to formulate and execute their own policies. When these prove unsuccessful, their services are not retained. The days when directors had any effec-tive voice in team selection have passed, although from time to time one hears of temporary revivals of the earlier practice, usually the result of an interregnum in the managership.

Little by little the mode of management of a major club has changed. Today, there are few secretary-managers, and where they exist it is not from choice but from financial stringency. The functions of the secretary of a First Division club approxi-mate closely to those of the secretary of an ordinary company. The secretary controls its varied business activities, assisted by a staff which must be familiar with modern office management, and from time to time he will have to call upon the services of a number of professional men—lawyers, accountants, tax special-ists, architects and surveyors. There will be dealings with departments of central government, with local authorities, with travel agencies and foreign football clubs, quite apart from the recurrent business of a busy club. All this is quite distinct from the work of a growing managerial staff, which will be concerned amongst other things with training, physical fitness, players' morale and welfare, team selection, the groundsman and his staff, and public relations. In place of old-type managers, who were a

species of maids-of-all-work for the board, there is now a leng-
thening chain of managerial posts, with clearly-differentiated
functions. An increasing number of clubs now possess a general
manager, who is immediately responsible to the board, and to
whom, in turn, all managerial staff and players are responsible.
Below him is the team manager, who in turn may have an assistant manager, a trainer and assistant trainer, a chief scout, a
physiotherapist and an indefinite number of lesser assistants.

Football management has now developed into a distinct profession and, indirectly, it has profited from the abolition of the
limit on players' wages in a variety of ways. In the first place,
the manager's salary has risen correspondingly with the increase
in wages. For a leading English club, it will range between
£5,000 and £10,000 a year, with liberal expenses. Secondly, the
very high running expenses of a first-class club has meant that
decisions affecting the playing success of the club must now be
left in the manager's hands. The playing of football at top level
is now so complex that the manager's expert views upon it can
scarcely be questioned. That is, however, the acid test. Success
today is almost everything, and every manager knows that if he
fails, he is out. The casualty rate among managers is very heavy,
even though it is axiomatic that, by the nature of the game, only
a few can expect to be successful. Today, successful managers,
and managers with a flair, are as eagerly sought as outstanding
players, and their achievements are, with few exceptions, almost
as uncertain. Not only by tradition, but of necessity, managers
are almost invariably selected from recently-retired players of
outstanding reputation. No-one else can expect to command the
confidence and support of the players sufficiently, and few others
would be in a position to decide whether the players are giving
the 100 per cent effort which the game always requires. No-one
has yet been able to analyse accurately in advance the factors
which go to the making of a successful manager. Celebrated
internationals have failed completely. Players who were relatively
unknown have proved to be brilliantly successful. There are
some managers who specialise in revivifying clubs which have

fallen on hard times. There are others who make a habit of guiding their clubs to promotion. Finally, there are the select few who can not only produce teams which, by general consent, are outstanding, but who can maintain them in perilous eminence, who can detect the first signs of decline, and arrest it by a timely replacement of players who have long entertained the public and who may have won all the honours which the game bestows, by young unknowns.

This latter task is the most difficult of all, especially when the close relationship between manager and long-service player is remembered, and it may bring surprises. Stanley Matthews played in Stoke City's first team at the age of seventeen. A quarter of a century later, when it appeared that his great playing career was drawing to a close, Stoke reluctantly released him to Blackpool where, with Stanley Mortensen, he appeared to renew his youth. Some years later still, when once again rumours of retirement circulated, Blackpool transferred him back to a faltering Stoke for a nominal £3,000. Once again the old magic worked. With his help, Stoke extricated themselves from trouble. Gates soared, and to everyone's surprise Matthews continued to play in their first team for several more seasons. One other example may be given. David Mackay, Tottenham Hotspur's Scottish international, suffered so serious an injury to his legs that it was thought that he would not play again. He was therefore acquired by Derby County on a free transfer, in order to add experience to a young and talented side. This, more than any other single factor, was responsible for Derby County's return to the First Division, and with them, David Mackay. With a talented replacement in MacFarland (already capped by England), Derby released him to Swindon. Obviously when he at length ceases to play, he will be able to select his managership.

This brief survey of modern football will have emphasised that very much is at stake every time a team takes the field. The rewards of success are very great, both for the club itself and for its players. Similarly, the consequences of failure can be disastrous. In this changed context, the old paternalism of football associations and leagues no longer has a place, more particularly since both clubs and players rely so much more today on the advice of experts. It is therefore not surprising that there is a marked tendency for both to test the extent of their rights in the courts. Until 1945, football amazingly had never been considered by Her Majesty's judges, except in one case, discussed below, which was considered so unimportant that it failed to find a place in the *Law Reports*. Today, on the contrary, rules are being tested, the conduct of officials challenged, and the whole framework of football is exposed to legal analysis. In this respect it resembles some other sports—for example, racing—where there have been similar actions. Until the *Eastham* decision, discussed later, it had not occurred to the footballer that the decisions of the Football Association and the Football League might be challenged—that behind them stood the courts and the machinery of the law, ready to exercise supervision in the interests of justice. How far that supervision extends may appear in the following chapters.

3
The Professional Football Club

With the exception of one club—Nottingham Forest—every club in membership with the Football League is a limited company. So are many lesser clubs, playing in a variety of lesser leagues; and, finally, so are a small number of amateur clubs. Whilst it is true that organisation into a limited liability company is the most convenient way of handling the affairs of a large club, it is also true that the company seems to have exercised a certain fascination over the minds of early football legislators, for both the Football Association and the Football League are limited liability companies, and the machinery for the transfer of shares on a transfer of membership is cumbrous and unusual.

The articles and memoranda of association of football clubs must fill outside persons with a feeling of wonder, for they bear no relation to modern company practice, and many give the impression that they were drafted on an offday in a fit of absence of mind—as perhaps they were. When the principal clubs incorporated last century, the books of precedents contained nothing resembling a precedent for a football club company—nor did they half a century later. The solicitor was therefore left to get along with instructions which were probably muddled, and were almost certainly complicated. Further, a number of incorporations occurred under earlier Companies Acts, and have probably not been brought up to date since. The structure of the company often reflected the wishes of the founders of the club. Some have a nominal capital—in at least one case, it is no more than £100. Clubs more recently incorporated may have a capital running into tens of thousands, but which is still out of line with the scale of the club. A number are private companies, with a restriction on the transfer of shares. In many cases, original shares have passed, through succession on death, into the hands of persons living far from the club's ground, and frequently with no interest in the club, or even in football. Quite often there is no formal transfer of these shares on the death of a holder, so that the establishment of present ownership may be a long and costly business, as the recent struggle to obtain a controlling interest in the Aston Villa club, in the period of its decline, sufficiently showed. Since a number of clubs have never paid a dividend, and many more are in arrears for a number of years, it is not surprising that the holders should be uninterested in them, if they also have no interest in the club. There is, in any case, no market for the shares in football clubs, and the sales which do take place are usually privately negotiated.

Why then should anyone be interested in acquiring or keeping shares? Two reasons may be suggested. The first is a genuine interest in the fortunes of the club, and although possession of a share may not bring much financial reward, it enables the owner to put in an appearance at the annual general meeting, and, if so inclined, to expound his views on the management of the club. Unlike other company meetings, comparatively little attention is given to matters of finance. Discussions concentrate upon the acquisition or non-acquisition of new players, upon poor performances of the club, and perhaps upon desirable improvements to the ground. Further, possession of a share may confer fringe benefits. Season tickets may be issued to owners of them in priority to ordinary members of the public, and so may tickets for Cup-ties (to which a season ticket does not extend), and if the club has an allocation of tickets for the Cup Final or for international matches, once again the shareholder is given priority in applications for them. Beyond that, the shareholder is of importance only when some person or group of persons wishes to acquire control of the club. It is on such occasions that the register of shareholders is anxiously searched, and is frequently discovered to be quite out of date. Since club balance sheets show that some clubs have not paid dividends for many years—and one or two, not at any time—the apathy of shareholders can be understood.

Club balance sheets will also show some other highly interesting features. Whilst in some clubs the capital is more or less evenly spread among the directors, who may be closely connected with the group of founders who created the clubs, in some others it is overwhelmingly concentrated in the hands of one person, or of two or three closely related persons. For example, four members of the Needler family (all directors) between them own approximately half the shares of Hull City—a club reconstituted after the war of 1939-45, with the unusually large number of 200,000 shares of 5s (25p) each. It is the leadership of the Needler family which has been largely the incentive for Hull City's playing successes in recent years. Everton, an outstandingly popular and successful club, has a capital comprising only 2,500 £1 shares, of which 898 are owned by Mr John Moore, the driving force in Littlewoods. The Mears family was largely responsible for the formation and success of Chelsea FC. They still own a large number of shares, and a third-generation member of the family is a director. Interestingly, the Dean family played a similar part in the foundation of Fulham FC, the ground being part of land owned by the Dean firm, and even today two members of the family are directors.

With the handicaps of a limited capital structure, often a restriction on transfer of shares, sometimes of shares in unwieldy denominations (eg, £20 or even £30) and an absence of any regularity in the payment of dividends so far as many clubs are concerned, there is naturally no question of any Stock Exchange quotation. There are also other reasons, which are to be found in the special rules of the Football Association applicable to football club companies. Since these have the appearance of something drawn from the Pentateuch, it will be well to consider them now, but first something must be said about the circumstances in which they were framed.

Originally, clubs whose names today are famous in the history of Association football were formed as voluntary associations, and the players were amateurs. The introduction of professionalism, which for a time was fiercely opposed, and the organisation of the

Football League, produced a host of new problems. Professional players needed contracts, their pay was regulated, and a formal system of registration and transfer was instituted. About the same time, a regular 'gate' was charged for admission to grounds which were becoming fully enclosed, and on which the first primitive stands were making their appearance. Football, in short, was becoming a business. This was regretted by some of the earlier pioneers of the game—for example, Lord Kinnaird and the brothers Clegg from Sheffield—but they had no alternative but to accept the changes. Nevertheless, they wished to alter as little as possible. Above all, they wished to prevent football becoming a sport which existed primarily for money-making or speculation. So far as was possible, they also wished to preserve the local character and intense municipal loyalty which has always characterised it. Finally, they drew a clear line between the amateur whom they still regarded as the backbone of the game, and the professional who, as a paid employee, reluctantly admitted, must be kept firmly in his place. Though the position of the player has altered completely in recent years, some marks of his earlier status remain.

These things may explain the special rules of the Football Association relating to club companies, and which are contained in Rule 45. They require that all articles of association should be approved by the Council, and that certain things must always be contained in them. These are:

1. A limitation on dividends paid to a maximum settled by the Football Association, and which has remained unchanged at $7\frac{1}{2}$ per cent or, if the dividend is paid tax free, at 5 per cent.

2 (a). So far as preference shares are concerned, the maximum is again $7\frac{1}{2}$ per cent, but if dividends on them are in arrear, this amount may be paid in respect of the past three years.

(b). A company may not issue more preference shares than the total of subscribed ordinary shares.

3. Shares may not be subdivided, and companies may not make a bonus issue or pay a capital dividend without the written consent of the Council.

Page 53 The spectators take over : a scene at Wembley during the 1923 Cup Final between West Ham and Bolton Wanderers

Page 54　Mounted police clear the pitch at Wembley before kick-off at the 1923 Cup Final

4. The company may not make a mortgage or charge upon its assets at a rate higher than $7\frac{1}{2}$ per cent without the written consent of the Football Association, and again, without the Association's consent a company may not borrow at a rate higher than $7\frac{1}{2}$ per cent. (Presumably this rule takes no account of bank overdrafts.)

5. A shareholder may buy a season ticket at a discount of 5 per cent, as compared with the charge to non-shareholders, any such ticket being non-transferable, except on death.

6. No director is entitled to receive any remuneration for acting as director or as an employee of the club.

7. A director is disqualified if he is suspended by the Football Association from taking part in football.

Rule 45 (a) continues:

(viii) *Winding-up of the Company* : On the winding-up of the Company the surplus assets shall be applied, first, in repaying to the Members the amount paid on their shares respectively, and if such assets shall be insufficient to repay the said amount in full, they shall be applied rateably, so that the loss shall fall upon the Members in proportion to the amount called up on their shares respectively, and no Member shall be entitled to call upon other Members for the purpose of adjusting his rights; but where any call has been made and has been paid by some of the Members such calls shall be enforced against the remaining Members for the purpose of adjusting the rights of the Members between themselves.

If the surplus assets shall be more than sufficient to pay to the Members the whole amount paid upon their shares, the balance shall be given to the Football Association Benevolent Fund, or to some other Club or Institute in the (city or county) having objects similar to those contained in the Memorandum of Association, or to any local charity, or charitable or benevolent institution situate within the said (city or county), such club, institute, or charity, to be decided upon and such property apportioned among all or any of such clubs, institutions, or charities by the Members of the Club, at or before the time of dissolution as they shall direct, or in default of any such decision or apportionment by the Members of the Club, the same to be decided upon and apportioned by a Judge of the High Court of

D

Justice having jurisdiction in such winding-up or dissolution and as he shall determine, or such balance may be disposed of in such other manner as the Members of the Club with the consent of the Council of the Football Association, if then existing, shall determine.

45 (b) *Memorandum and Articles—Changes.*

In addition to the above it is a condition of membership of the Association that the proposed Memorandum and Articles of Association of any new Company and any proposed change or changes in the Memorandum or Articles of an existing Company shall be lodged at the Offices of the Football Association at least fourteen days before it is proposed they should become operative or submitted for approval to a General Meeting of Shareholders.

There is also a third section (c) which deals with three minor matters.

Much of this rule is now quite out of line with modern company practice. For example, however occasional football club dividends may be, their limitation to $7\frac{1}{2}$ per cent places the return on either ordinary shares as speculative as these, or on preference shares, well below the market rate, whilst subsection (iv) whatever its effect may be (and that is not altogether clear) places mortgages and allied transactions, as a purely commercial operation, for practical purposes, beyond the reach of a club company. There is, however, a more serious objection to this subsection (and also to others eg, in Rule 40). These transactions require the consent of the Council, and when the composition of the Council is discussed later (in Chapter Four), it will be apparent that, even assuming professional advice, this is scarcely the body to make informed decisions on matters of this importance.

Another subsection prevents directors from receiving any remuneration for acting. Obviously this is a late survival of amateurism, and quite out of line with modern thinking. At a time when players and managers are remunerated on a scale undreamt of twenty or thirty years ago, it would seem particularly inappropriate. It has certainly discouraged a number of business men from entering into the management of football, and if it should be asserted that football has no need for the services of such men, it stands in lonely isolation from the rest of the business world. The affairs of a leading club today are not only business, but big business—sometimes very big business—and it is almost axiomatic that such business would be more efficiently handled if the experts were encouraged to participate more extensively.

With subsection (viii) of Rule 45 we enter a strange half-world, in which Her Majesty's judges make a fleeting appearance of uncertain duration, in a confused account of several possible methods of disposing of surplus assets on the dissolution of a club company. It is possibly a good thing that one can recall no instance where a club company in dissolution was in the fortunate position of possessing surplus assets. The first paragraph of the subsection is in any case irrelevant, for the Winding-up Section of the Companies Act, 1948, governs the procedure and application of assets on a dissolution, and this subsection obviously cannot modify it. The second paragraph is confused, and might, if applied, produce some strange results. If the calamity should ever occur that Everton FC were wound up, its assets might conceivably be allotted to Liverpool FC—a result which might well have some repercussions on Merseyside. The capital value of a freehold ground in the centre of a city may now be so large that a voluntary winding-up might produce some highly interesting results. Of course, one knows that, in practice, where this occurs, it is usual for a new organisation to come into existence, and that this new organisation will make a claim to any surplus assets; but the paragraph abounds with alternatives, and conflicting interests are likely to be severely pressed.

The truth of the matter is that Rule 45 belongs to the nineteenth century, not to the twentieth. Much of it should be scrapped, in order that clubs should enjoy greater freedom to raise the money needed to modernise their organisation and amenities. In a case which will be discussed later, this question has already attained some prominence, but a good deal more will be heard of it in the future.

For many years also Rule 31 contained a bleak provision which excluded not only a professional player, but anyone who at any time, *had been* a professional player, from serving on the council of the Football Association or any of its committees, or on the board of committee of any league, club or association. Nor could any such person represent his own or any other association, league or club at any football meeting. How far this astonishing rule was observed in its entirety is unknown, but its existence has excluded, particularly from boards of directors of professional clubs, many of those best qualified to serve on them. Fortunately, this rule has now been qualified. A professional player is still excluded, but the disabilities of those who have ceased to play have been removed, and one may hope that the accession of Sir Matt Busby to the board of Manchester United on relinquishing all his managerial duties in June 1971 inaugurated a new and more enlightened era. Earlier, in 1965, the club board had made a special issue of shares worth £12,000 to mark Sir Matt's completion of twenty years' service with Manchester United. The value of those services may in part be estimated by recalling that during those two decades, Manchester United won the League Championship five times, they were runners-up seven times; they won the FA Cup twice; the European Cup once; the FA Youth Cup six times; and finally, the FA Charity Shield five times. Most of all Sir Matt's managership will be remembered for the re-creation of the club after the Munich air disaster, in which eight members of the team were killed and he himself was very seriously injured.

It has been mentioned several times that the affairs of a major club are now big business. How big is the business, and where does the money go? Before this question can be answered, it is first necessary to say something of the changed functions and responsibilities of the modern director who, it should be remembered, is giving his services free—and is frequently denounced by sports writers in the popular press for his pains. Unlike players and managers, directors are rarely pursued by journalists, who tend to regard them as faceless nonentities, ignorant of the game and with minds firmly set against progress.

The reality is utterly different. If directors were really as the journalists tend to see them, they would never have become involved with football at all. For them, unlike the players, there are no financial rewards, and practically never any approval. Their successes pass virtually unnoticed. Their failures are pilloried. They are only news when they are so sharply divided in the boardroom that possible resignations stir public interest. Where boards are small, and one director owns a very large block of shares, such a division cannot exist, and accordingly the news value of such a board is nil. So far as the successful clubs of today are concerned, one might gather the impression from the press that they consisted only of players and the manager's staff; but behind them is a board of directors whose good judgement and attention to the best interests of the clubs have planned the success story.

This may be illustrated by the rise of two recent additions to the Football League—Oxford United and Cambridge United. At the end of the 1939-45 war, Oxford United (then Headington United) was an amateur club, only recently admitted to senior status, playing in Division I (ie, the second) of the Spartan League. They played on an open ground in a suburb, and ranked far behind Oxford's historic amateur club, Oxford City, members of the Isthmian League and winners of the Amateur Cup. Nevertheless, the Headington committee decided to turn the club into a professional club, as a limited company, and since the Southern League at that time was contemplating forming a Second Division, they applied for admission to it. Gradually, however, support for the Second Division dwindled, until only two of the applicants remained—Headington United and Weymouth. The Southern League resolved the problem by extending its membership to twenty-four, and admitting both clubs. Thereafter, Headington's story in the Southern League was one of almost unbroken success. At the same time, the directors (who were mainly the old club committee) had energetically pursued a policy of ground development, which eventually made the ground one of the very best in the Southern League. When

Accrington Stanley were unable to continue, the succession of Oxford United (the name having been changed during the club's brilliant career in the Southern League) had a look of inevitability about it; and those who know the dedication of the Oxford board have not been surprised that (again in a very brief time) the club has risen to the Second Division. When full tribute has been paid to the keenness of manager and players, the fact remains that the decisive factor in the rise of Oxford United has been the enthusiasm of its board of directors, backed by the confidence of the club's supporters.

The story of Cambridge United has been strikingly similar. They, too, at the end of the war were an amateur club, playing in Division I of the Spartan League, under the name of Abbey United. Once again, an enthusiastic committee was responsible for its change to professional status as a limited company, at the same time joining the Southern League, where they were also very successful. Their election to Division IV of the Football League is more recent than that of Oxford United, but a board of directors which has taken them so far is not likely to relax its efforts now.

The Football League is sometimes criticised for its reluctance to admit new members, and it is certainly true that its composition continues to be remarkably stable. One reason is that the directors who represent clubs at League meetings know, as press and public do not, of the unremitting struggles which clubs make to remain in existence and to retain their League status (which, once lost, is extraordinarily difficult to recover). In general, the League will only refuse to vote a member back again if it is convinced that its board is either unequal to the effort or has lost its enthusiasm. Collectively, the clubs also know that every possible local effort will be made before a League club fails.

The list of club directors shows that present-day boards include a fair sprinkling of solicitors, doctors and chartered accountants, although the majority are, naturally, local business men. Recently, a little gimmickry has crept in with the appointment of prominent television stars. A substantial number of directors also serve as aldermen or municipal councillors, or as Justices of the Peace, a bent towards local service being responsible for both activities. Fortunately, party politics have no place in football and the occasional efforts of politicians to obtain a little free publicity by showing interest have been coolly received.

Balance sheets of the League clubs reveal the widest variations in modes of operation, and they frequently fly warning signals for those which are struggling. At the other end of the scale, however, the receipts and expenditure of one of the foremost clubs must seem to the less fortunate something like a fairy tale, even though it still falls far short of the expenditure of leading continental clubs, more especially of Italian clubs, and of those of South America, and especially of Brazil. The same balance sheets also show, not only remarkable differences in the scale of expenditure as between clubs of apparently comparable performance, but also the quite extraordinary reliance of the club for solvency upon gate receipts. More will be said on this question in a later chapter, but it may be stated as a general proposition that it is this factor, more than any other, which conditions the remuneration and acquisition of players, and ultimately the club's performance. Even if a club temporarily embarks upon a bold spending policy in the hope of improving its status, then unless it is quite unusually successful in the extent to which it attracts additional support, this will have to be balanced, before too long a time has elapsed, by a transfer of talented players for a substantial fee, in order to reduce the overdraft. In embarking upon a spending policy, not all clubs are in the fortunate position of owning the freehold of their ground, so making it possible for them to offer security for their overdraft. Most frequently this must be guaranteed by the directors themselves, often with no security at all. This makes both club and directors vulnerable to periodic credit squeezes, and to higher interest rates for loans. It is quite astonishing that even today the ordinary commercial ways of raising additional money are still not available to the directors of football clubs. Where the purses of the directors fail, the club's only other recourse is normally to the supporters' club. Today, few clubs except those at the very summit of the League can afford to operate without them, and often the preservation of harmonious relations with a supporters' club is an important part of the task of the chairman of a club.

Whether the board remains in close contact with its supporters' club or not, its very existence increases the responsibilities of those who guide the fortunes of the football club it serves. Rule 44 (e) of the Association provides that a club may not accept financial assistance from its supporters' club unless it obtains from the supporters' club an undertaking that it will strictly observe the requirements of Rule 25. This is a long and complicated rule designed to prevent direct or indirect approaches to amateur players in other than the appropriate way. It is, as we shall see, yet another effort to control the offer of unpermitted inducements to such players—and it is as ineffective as earlier efforts to check them have been. Rule 44 (e) also requires that the accounts of supporters' clubs shall be made available to the Football Association or an affiliated county association, with details showing that no improper payments have been made directly or indirectly to any amateur player. This rule, it will be seen, has virtually no relevance to the supporters' club of any professional football club, but such supporters' clubs are often fundamental to the continued existence of an amateur club. In the professional world, some fortunate and wealthy clubs still operate with little direct contact with a supporters' club. Those who need such support often direct its money-raising activities towards ground improvement or the acquisition of specified players. To do more would expose the club to the risk of control from the supporters. This, it might appear, would operate to the detriment of the football club itself, yet in a number of cases the danger is more apparent than real, for the most active members of the supporters' club are usually the shareholders of the football club.

The modern profit and loss accounts and balance sheets of typical Football League clubs show the utmost extremes of prosperity and poverty. In the season 1967-68, Manchester United (by common consent one of the most colourful and successful clubs of modern times) won the European Cup, and did well in League and Cup. Enthusiasm and support remained high throughout the season, more especially as this was the year in which the club's ever-popular manager received a knighthood. The average attendance at home games was over 57,000 a match. The club has a nominal capital of £15,000, of which £5,859 has been subscribed. It owns the Old Trafford ground, which appears in the balance sheet valued at just over £500,000, which is far below its actual value. In addition, the club owns dwelling-houses (mainly acquired for the occupation of players) to the value of over £50,000. Gate receipts amounted to no less than £530,800, from which approximately £75,000 should be deducted, as payments to visiting clubs, the Football League and the Football Association. In comparison with these receipts all others (programmes, TV facilities etc) were quite trifling, nor did transfer fees, either given or received, play any part in the club's financial status. This, of course, was due to the shrewdness with which the manager selected and trained young players, and to the fact that a successful side is also, apart from injuries, a settled side.

As against these exceptionally high receipts, players' wages and bonuses accounted for over £194,000 of expenses, to which must be added nearly £40,000 in travelling and hotel expenses, match expenses, insurance, equipment and similar items, the whole of this part of the expenditure amounting to £280,794, out of a total expenditure of £385,066. It will therefore be apparent that there was a surplus in the year's working of £107,104. Not unnaturally, the club paid a dividend of $7\frac{1}{2}$ per cent on its preference shares and 5 per cent on its ordinary shares, and this consumed the vast sum of £481 4s 1d. The remainder was carried forward to an accumulated balance surplus which, being in excess of £455,544 after taxation, not only provides a reserve fund of considerable size, but also supplies the finance for the repayment of the cost of the substantial improvements which have been carried out on the ground. So long as the club continues to be as successful as these figures show it to be, it has no need to consider how to supplement its income by auxiliary activities.

In the season 1968-69, the club's receipts reached a total of £648,078, and in 1969-70 they amounted to £620,155, but deductions for visiting clubs, shares of Cup-tie receipts, and payments to associations were substantially larger. In both seasons this was due to outstanding success in Cup competitions. In each year also there was a substantial profit, amounting to £65,201 in 1969, and to £44,949 in 1970. What is perhaps most significant in these figures is that, in spite of continuing success at the highest level, the profit margin even of Manchester United has tended to diminish, whilst players' wages and bonuses have continued to increase. In 1970, for example, they amounted to £230,180.

The accounts of Everton for the year 1968-69 showed a comparable though slightly less spectacular strength. The year to which they referred had been a successful one. The club reached the semi-final of the FA Cup, and finished third in the League. In addition, it competed in the Inter-Cities Fairs Cup Competition, one of several European competitions. Everton, too, has undertaken very substantial ground improvements in recent years. The attendances at Everton's home games were not far below those of Manchester United, and the total income, after deduction of the percentage of the gate due to visitors, the League and associations, and the share of Cup-tie receipts to which visitors in Cup matches are entitled, was strikingly similar to that of Manchester United, being £463,052. This included £38,000 in transfer fees. Of the expenditure, over £102,177 was paid in players' wages (including bonuses and benefits) and £16,790 in travel and match expenses—a much smaller amount than Manchester United paid. On the other hand, Everton appropriated no less than £188,202 to ground expenses and maintenance. This was due primarily in respect of the expenses of constructing the new and impressive modern stand in Goodison Road. Even after all expenses had been met, there still remained a profit of £56,967. This was transferred to accumulated reserve to cover future ground improvements and possible payments of transfer fees. No dividend was paid, but since the total capital of Everton FC, both nominal and issued, amounts only to £2,500, of which two directors own £1,167, the fact that no dividend was paid is scarcely relevant.

The accounts of Everton for the following two seasons, ending in 1970 and 1971, show a similar healthiness to those of Manchester United, even though in a playing sense Everton were during this period rather less successful. Although their income is composed slightly differently from that of Manchester United, it continued to rise, to an extent directly comparable with that of their Manchester rivals. So also did players' wages, which in 1970 totalled £149,162, and in 1971 £177,687. These figures do not mean that Everton players are paid less generously than those of Manchester United, but rather that, having been less successful, there were fewer bonuses paid, and fewer matches played. Once again, the margin of profit is seen to be lower. It amounted to £30,611 in 1970, and to £25,562 in 1971. This is, in reality, a small margin with so large a turnover.

In spite of the heavy rebuilding which both these popular clubs have undertaken, both have very large reserves with which to face any possible future change of fortune. So long as they retain their popularity, the provision of extra accommodation in modern stands will again bring an increase of income. At the same time, the conspicuous success of the training policy of both clubs has made resort to heavy transfer fees a rarity. Finally, the playing records and finances of both clubs illustrate the remarkable results which can be achieved through close co-operation between board, manager and players.

If one turns to the Second Division, the figures show a very marked diminution, even for the most successful members. Except locally, the players are not so well-known, they rarely appear in international matches, and the clubs appear only rarely in Cup Finals. If there is a successful First Division club within easy reach by motor-car, the Second Division club's support may expect to suffer from the superior power of attraction of its rival. This situation, nevertheless, may be reversed if the rival is floundering towards the bottom of the First Division, and the club itself is making a bid for promotion which has placed it among the top three or four clubs of the Division. At such a time the increase in support is very great.

Two clubs which in recent years have always been among the promotion aspirants in the Second Division are Sheffield United and Hull City. In the season 1970-71, in the latter part of which seven or eight clubs were engaged in one of the most stubbornly-contested promotion battles in the history of the League, Sheffield United (with Leicester City) were successful, and Hull City failed during the last weeks of the season by a narrow margin. In other respects, the two clubs may be sharply contrasted. Sheffield United has a long tradition of membership in the First Division. Hull City has never quite reached it, although few doubt that it will in the near future. Sheffield is one of the birthplaces of Association football; there is no Rugby League club, and no Rugby Union of note. Competition, therefore, exists only from Sheffield Wednesday, themselves suffering eclipse, and from lesser clubs in the vicinity, such as Rotherham United, Barnsley, Doncaster Rovers and Chesterfield, all of whom at some period have been Second Division clubs. Hull City, on the other hand, faces competition from two popular and frequently highly successful Rugby League clubs. It is possible to pursue the contrast further. Sheffield United play upon an old-fashioned ground (now being modernised) which is shared with cricket. Sheffield United cricket club play there, and so does Yorkshire—with the result that the football pitch has an open side to the cricket area. One imagines that this may slightly affect players, and it certainly limits the income which can be obtained from season tickets for accommodation under cover. Something more will be said on this in the chapter in which grounds are discussed. Hull City, on the other hand, lost their original ground at Anlanby Road during the war and began again at

Boothferry Park, which is already a finely-appointed ground. Finally, it may be said that the board of Sheffield United contains no member, or two or three members, who occupy the dominating position that the Needler family does in respect of Hull City.

Bearing these factors in mind, the differences between the profit and loss accounts and the balance sheets of these two successful Second Division clubs and those of the two successful First Division clubs are of great interest. In the year ending in April 1969, the Hull City club had an accumulated loss from previous years of £161,606, to which £6,415 was added in 1969. Sums paid to visiting clubs, association and other fees were approximately the same, and so were wages, salaries, travelling and other expenses. Indeed, the totals on these items showed a reduction from £93,383 to £84,749. There were also small reductions on other expenses, so that the total expenditure on these items was reduced from £177,073 in 1968 to £144,148 in 1969. Part of this was due to the absence of any sum in respect of transfer fees paid, although on the other side of the ledger the sums received from transfers was reduced from £7,000 to £3,000. Receipts for the year had also declined somewhat. The gross sum paid for admission in 1969 was £97,549, as compared with £109,010 the year before. Shares of gates in away matches had declined by £4,000, reflecting the general reduction in Second Division attendances, and £20,000 less had been received from three funds raised by the supporters, but earmarked for the development of the ground and for the acquisition of new players. These factors were sufficient to turn the small profit of £4,260 for 1968 into a small loss for 1969, on a total expenditure of only about one-third the amount of a successful First Division club. Incidentally, in such a balance sheet, the amount paid in wages and salaries in 1969 amounted to slightly more than one-half the total expenditure. Naturally, no dividend was paid.

In the following two seasons, Hull City continued their unsuccesful attempt to reach the First Division, and this is reflected in their balance sheets for 1970 and 1971. The accumulated debit balance grew to £179,589 in 1970, and again to £191,931 in 1971. Wages, salaries, travelling, house accommodation and ancillary expenses show an increase to £88,098 in 1970, and a marked increase to £123,668 in 1971. In addition, in 1971, there was an additional net expenditure of over £100,000 on transfer fees. Since other charges also increased in consequence primarily of inflation, the balance sheet of 1971 would have had a much more sombre appearance had it not been for the fact that gross paid admission received, which slumped to £77,702 in 1970, rose to £202,905, chiefly because Hull City in that season were involved in a race for promotion which remained undecided until the last few weeks of the season.

The revenue account of Sheffield United for 1967 is made up differently from that of Hull City, primarily because it also covers a modest expenditure on cricket, and also the income derived from it. Also the expense of the ground and general administration are not apportioned between the two sports. Taking these things roughly into account, the accounts show that the total expenditure on football was slightly less than that of Hull City, being just under £150,000, of which £63,547 was paid in players' wages, this being almost exactly the same as the year before. In a playing sense, the season was not a particularly successful one, for the club was rapidly dismissed from both the FA Cup and the League Cup, and finished low in the First Division, being relegated to the Second two seasons later. Approximately £9,000 was raised by supporters, primarily for the usual purposes, and a modest profit of £6,306 was shown— rather less than half that of the year before. On this, the club paid the full dividend of $7\frac{1}{2}$ per cent on the preference shares— a tribute to shrewd management. The financial picture of course changed completely with Sheffield United's promotion to the First Division in 1971.

In contrast with Hull City, Sheffield United gained promotion in 1971. Nevertheless, the similarities in the financial experience of these two clubs during 1970 and 1971 are more striking than their differences. Wages paid at Sheffield in 1970 amounted to £78,876; in 1971 they had risen to £114,377. In 1970, Sheffield United received nearly £60,000 in transfer fees. In 1971, in order to strengthen the team for promotion, they incurred an expenditure of £49,659 on transfers. In 1970, the gate receipts (including season tickets) amounted to slightly over £120,000. In 1971, because of the sustained interest in promotion, they had risen to £177,123. On the other hand, whilst the club showed a profit of £19,015 in 1970, there was a loss of £53,407 in 1971, and accordingly no dividend was paid. The experience of both clubs therefore shows that there is a price to be paid for attempting promotion, whether successful or not.

The accounts of these two clubs, both of which have a distinguished Second Division record show: (i) how much more limited the receipts, and therefore the expenditure, are in the Second Division; and (ii) that supporters' clubs are not only of great importance in maintaining interest, but also make a significant contribution to the running even of good Second Division clubs. Finally, it may be pointed out that the more restricted scale of operation shows not only why clubs are so anxious to gain, or to retain, First Division status, but also one reason why many players are ready to leave a Second Division club for the First. With no maximum wage, rewards can be altogether greater, thus leading in turn to an increasing tendency to concentrate talent in the most successful clubs in the First Division.

In the season 1967-68, Bury and Northampton Town were both in the Third Division. Bury is an old-established club, which once won the FA Cup and for a few seasons after the first world war held a place in the First Division. With the counter-attractions of the two great Manchester clubs on its doorstep, and several other League clubs not very far away, it has always been a struggle for Bury to exist. Northampton Town, on the other hand, is situated in a growing town with no very close rivals. It joined the old Third Division (South) from the Southern League, and a few seasons ago climbed briefly to the First, only to be relegated after a single unhappy season. Like their nearest neighbours, Luton Town, their descent was swift and inglorious, and again like Luton's, it also involved a period in the Fourth Division. Yet, in spite of these misfortunes, the club in 1969 was able to show a profit of £15,381 on the year, which went to reduce accumulated losses of £27,665. This profit, as the directors' report pointed out, was due to the contributions from supporters, practically the whole of which was spent on transfer fees. The total receipts amounted to £128,900 and the expenses to £143,894, of which players' wages accounted for £67,437. The receipts are therefore less, but the expenses are roughly the same, as those of a Second Division club. Northampton Town play on the county ground, so that very little in respect of ground improvement was possible or necessary, and only maintenance of it therefore appears in the accounts.

At the end of the 1969-70 season, the situation became somewhat worse. Receipts for admission were virtually identical with those of the year before, but expenses had risen to £179,776, the great bulk of which was due to increased wages, ground expenses, and an increase in transfer fees paid from £23,000 in 1969 to £42,000 in 1970. In this year, therefore, there was a net loss of £47,194, which raised the accumulated loss, which had been substantially diminished in 1969, to £59,478. It is evident that, at this level, even modest success in cup competitions can make a substantial difference to the final figures.

The Bury club has, of necessity, always been very prudently managed, and its accounts for 1969 show this prudence abundantly. The expenses of the club were slightly less than those of Northampton Town, being £130,999, with players' wages and staff salaries accounting for £67,613. It is however on the other side of the account that the comparison with Northampton Town is most interesting. Northampton Town, it has been stated, paid £23,000 in transfer fees, but against that they received £23,500. Their gross gate receipts were £47,895. Gate receipts at Bury were very much the same—£46,808, and they, too, had important gifts from the supporters, and profits from the social

Page 71
A general view of
Wembley Stadium
as spectators begin
to gather for the
community singing
which precedes a
Cup Final

Page 72 The Aztec Stadium in Mexico City, which has accommodation for 200,000 spectators

club. However, their profit was no less than £42,340—a remarkable figure which is almost completely explained by the fact that they received £54,818 in transfer fees, and paid out nothing for the acquisition of other players.

The accounts of Bury FC for 1970 and 1971, like those of Northampton Town, show the very real difficulties of clubs in lower divisions even with the most careful management. Expenditure on players' wages has varied only slightly. They rose to £68,433 in 1970, but actually declined to £65,354 in 1971. Gate receipts (including season tickets) totalled no more than £32,258, in 1970, but improved to £34,847 in 1971. Even so, it is clear that competition from Manchester is acute. The Bury balance sheets show losses both in 1970 and 1971, although in 1971 it was as little as £558, with an accumulated loss amounting to £47,443.

The accounts of two casually-selected Fourth Division clubs, Doncaster Rovers and Wrexham (the latter being in 1969-70 among the four promoted to the Third Division) again show the diminishing scale of operations. The capital of Doncaster Rovers consists of 10,000 10s shares, all issued. The profit and loss account for 1969 showed gross receipts of £69,571—this comparatively high figure being explained by the fact that the substantial sum of £16,392 was taken for Cup-ties and friendly matches. On the other hand, the sale of season tickets produced only £1,625. At Third and Fourth Division matches (excluding Cup-ties) there need be no anxiety about a seat in the stand. Wages and management salaries totalled £64,655, and match and travelling expenses £6,266. There was an adverse balance on transfer fees of £6,500, and it is noteworthy that the amount of £3,247 spent on ground maintenance and repairs is almost exactly the same as that spent on stationery, postage, advertising and similar expenses. Doncaster Rovers rent their ground from the council and they are therefore only indirectly concerned with its development. Nevertheless, the year showed a net loss of £18,393, which (as the annual report pointed out) was mainly through payment of transfer fees, and reduced donations from

E

supporters. The expenditure on transfers would scarcely have been noticed by a successful First Division club, which would also have not needed to rely on gifts from supporters' organisations.

The total expenditure of the Wrexham Club in the same year very closely approximated to that of Doncaster Rovers—£88,957 as against £89,062. The Wrexham ground is also leased, and the cost of rent, rates and repairs did not differ markedly from those incurred at Doncaster. Players' wages and managerial salaries, however, accounted for considerably less—£43,413, as compared with £64,655. The adverse balance of transfer fees was also less, amounting to £2,300. As a result of most careful management, the club was able to show a profit of £12,458, which was carried forward, no dividend being paid. Relatively, Wrexham were in a much healthier position than Doncaster Rovers, the accumulated balance amounting to £61,428.

The Wrexham balance sheets for the two following years, 1970 and 1971, again exhibit the great but unavailing efforts made to keep down expenditure in face of inflation. In 1970, the total expenditure was £112,271. In 1971, it actually declined a little to £109,907. This was due almost entirely to the fact that players' wages, which had risen to £52,829 in 1970, were reduced (by pruning the playing strength) to £47,518 in 1971. Gate receipts remained practically constant. They were £52,795 in 1970 and £58,427 in 1971, although receipts from Cup matches and the Cup pools of the Football Association and of the League raised this figure to £86,178 in 1970 and to £85,714 in 1971. Once again the Wrexham position remained comparatively healthy, there being a profit of £15,149 in 1970, and one of £12,983 in 1971.

A number of points appear from this analysis of balance sheets of typical clubs in all four divisions of the League. The first is that the capital of a club bears no relation to the scale of its activities. Some of the largest and most prosperous have a capital so small as to be almost negligible. Further, many clubs have paid no dividend for years, and where they have made a profit, it has often been held as a reserve against future difficulties. Again, whilst the profits of a successful First Division club may be very large, the line between profit and loss in the Third and Fourth Divisions is a very narrow one. Further, whilst the operations of supporters' clubs and associations are relatively insignificant at First Division level, they begin to appear in the finances of Second Division clubs, and they are of considerable and growing importance to the football club itself at Third and Fourth Division level. Another significant feature is that, whilst most of the First and many of the Second Division clubs (most of which are also the oldest League clubs) own their grounds and therefore have a direct interest in the improvement of them, a substantial number of clubs in the two lower divisions operate on grounds which are leased, most frequently from the local authority, so that, in general, they are chiefly concerned in keeping them in sound condition—and the money available for this is often very small.

Yet another interesting point is that transfer fees are rarely of importance in the balance sheets of the humbler clubs. Now that training schemes are fully developed among the major clubs and their effectiveness may be tested by performance in the FA Youth Cup and other youth competitions, resort to the lower divisions for a player tends to become less frequent. There is obviously no real hope of salvation for a struggling club in such a deal, more especially as promising youths increasingly seek to be signed on by major clubs, where not only are the rewards higher, but also the general level of training. This may be carried a step further. Below the Fourth Division, there is a considerable number of professional clubs playing in leagues of high standing and long reputations, the most notable being the Southern and Midland Leagues, the Cheshire League, and the Lancashire Combination. For them, the struggle for existence is even harder, for ground maintenance and running costs approach those of the Fourth Division clubs, whilst attendances range from 1,500 to 3,000 for ordinary league matches. The professionals of these clubs are almost exclusively part-time players, and the wages bill is therefore very much less. For them, a successful season is one in which the club enjoys a good Cup run, terminating with an away fixture against a First or Second Division club. Early dismissal from the FA Cup competition means flagging interest and declining attendances.

Since the capital of a club bears no meaningful relation to its activities, and since dividends are in any case limited to $7\frac{1}{2}$ per cent and tend to be something of a rarity even when a profit is shown, it can be affirmed with some confidence that no-one invests in the shares of a football club for financial gain. The original motive was an interest in, and a desire to support, the football club, and even this may have been confined to a fairly small group. As the years have passed and the original shareholders have died, shares may have passed to those who have no interest in football, or who have removed to some other part of the country. Sometimes they are even held, as it were by inadvertence, by enthusiastic supporters of some other club. Herein lies a danger for the struggling club. Something new is needed to rekindle flagging interest, and this is a point which will be considered further in a later chapter.

One may wonder why it is that people are willing to work hard without rewards as directors of football clubs. If things go wrong, they are expected to lend money (free of interest) to the club, and to guarantee bank loans in emergencies. To the public, they remain individually anonymous, and in the press they are frequently accused of obstructing managers and being opposed to change. It will be fully evident from the figures given in this chapter that, except at the highest level, directors have often little room for manoeuvre and have no choice but to scrutinise very closely any proposal which may disturb the delicate balance on which they work. For some, doubtless, being a director is something of a gamble—comparable perhaps with being the owner of a string of mediocre racehorses. For others, it may be regarded as a civic duty. Others again have reluctantly agreed to serve because they are directors of industries with large local employment, and something of the old, paternalistic attitude still survives. For most nevertheless, the major (and not infrequently, the sole reason) is that they love the game, almost to the point of obsession, and feel that they can make a contribution to it.

A survey of the finances of clubs in lower divisions over a longer period would have shown that there is a tendency for attendances to decline, especially in the latter part of the season. It is not so much bad weather, as lack of purpose, which is mainly responsible. Both the Football Association and the Football League are conscious of this, and have done something to improve the position. Recently, the Football Association introduced a knock-out tournament for professional non-League clubs, and this is gradually arousing a growing interest among the supporters of the clubs who, because they do not appear in the forms of football pools, very rarely attract other than local publicity. It is remarkable that this tournament is the first (other than the qualifying competition for the FA Cup itself) which has brought together professional clubs from these leagues. One might have thought that, having failed to secure an automatic exchange between their league champions and the lowest clubs in Division Four, they might themselves have promoted a premier division on national lines. After all, the applicants for admission to the Fourth Division in any year would make a fair nucleus for such a division. Some names appear year by year, and the clubs must have considered the cost very carefully. No such development has occurred, however.

Two recent innovations of the Football League must also be mentioned. The first is the introduction of the Football League Cup, now a highly successful competition whose final tie fills the Wembley Stadium. Already it has achieved a character of its own. There has been much comment upon the fact that, although in its long history the FA Cup has never been won by a Third or Fourth Division club, in the ten years of its life the Football League Cup has twice been won by a member of the Third Division. In 1967 Queen's Park Rangers defeated West Bromwich Albion, and in 1969 Swindon Town defeated the Arsenal. Although there was at first a manifest tendency on the part of some First Division clubs to regard this tournament lightly, this is no longer so, and even for them it has proved a valuable addition to the exchequer. One reason for the success of the Third Division clubs in this competition is the way in which the two competitions are arranged. The FA Cup competition has always been a really national tournament, in which virtually all senior clubs, whether professional or amateur, participate. Before the competition proper begins, there is a series of qualifying rounds, arranged in progressively expanding local areas, through which a limited number of the professional non-League clubs and amateur clubs struggle to the first round proper, at which point the members of the Third and Fourth Divisions enter. These clubs play the first two rounds, and the survivors, now reduced to twenty, join the forty-four clubs of the First and Second Divisions. The FA Cup is therefore weighted heavily against members of the Third and Fourth Divisions. In the Football League Cup, on the other hand, entries are confined to the members of all four divisions, and in the earlier rounds they are paired in a number of areas. All clubs, therefore, have an equal chance, of which two Third Division clubs (both of which reached higher status shortly afterwards) availed themselves to the full.

A further step forward was taken by the League in 1971, when it gave approval to a new knock-out competition for Third and Fourth Division clubs. It is intended that the competition should operate in the second half of the season, by which time these clubs will (with extremely rare exceptions) have ceased to be concerned with the FA Cup competition, and the prospects of promotion will have vanished for the majority of clubs. This new competition will, therefore, be a means of retaining interest in the fortunes of clubs which function far from the limelight, and it may make a substantial contribution towards their increasingly stretched finances.

4
Football Grounds

The development of international football, and particularly the extension of matches and competitions to Latin America, have familiarised English audiences through television and the popular press with football clubs which possess stadiums and amenities far outranging any in the British Isles. The supreme examples of modern engineering skill in the building of them are the vast stadium in Rio de Janeiro, the capacity of which is approximately 220,000, and the equally impressive stadium in Mexico City, accommodating 200,000, in which the final and some of the games in the World Cup series were played. Their enormous size is by no means the only feature which excels anything to be found in this country, or even in Europe. They are completely modern in conception. Built in the form of a vast oval, each of these giants has an upper tier, surmounted by roofing which completely surrounds the arena. Seen from the air they express a harmony which no European headquarters can approach, and when viewed from inside it is found that they are so constructed that there are very few unsightly pillars to obstruct the vision of spectators. Further, spectators are seated in every part of the ground, and partly for this reason receipts from important matches can reach staggering sums, completely dwarfing the £120,000 which is now paid to watch the final of the FA Cup.

The amenities of such a stadium are on a similarly lavish scale. Approaches to the tiers of seating are broad and easy, and resemble those of a great opera-house more closely than those of grounds in the British Isles—even First Division grounds. In the sweeping entrances there are restaurants, bars, shops and amusements of many kinds. Above all, the comfort of the players has been closely studied, and their accommodation again surpasses that of any British club. At Rio, the stadium even includes sleeping-quarters for players, as well as a full range of medical equipment and facilities for both indoor and outdoor training, including table-tennis and many other indoor pastimes. The clubs who have the good fortune to play in such luxurious conditions frequently have attached to them club facilities for all —whether supporters of the club or not—who can gain admittance to them. Membership, though expensive, is eagerly sought. The revenues of the football club, together with membership dues, finance the construction and maintenance of tennis courts and swimming pools, and these sports clubs have become the rendezvous of the more prosperous citizens, and particularly of their younger members. The football club can well afford to subsidise these activities, for they make the club itself the centre of local life and the achievements of its players a matter of civic, and even of national pride. Football in Latin America is followed by all classes with a fanaticism that approaches religious fervour.

Although these two stadiums stand at the summit of structural achievement, there are a number of others which are in the same class from the standpoint of amenities, and Brazil alone possesses several with a capacity of 100,000 or slightly more.

The contrast to European and United Kingdom football grounds is sharp. In the whole of the British Isles, there are only two which can accommodate a six-figure crowd. The English one is Wembley, the capacity of which is now slightly in excess of 100,000, and Hampden Park, Glasgow, the home of Queen's Park, a club which was one of the first entrants for the FA Cup, which has never wavered in its attachment to the amateur game, but which now lingers in the obscurity of the Second Division, watched by a crowd of 3-4,000. Hampden Park once had an attendance of 164,000, but since 1945 under a stricter survey for the safety of spectators, the maximum has been fixed at 135,000, a figure which is closely approached for international matches and for the finals of the Scottish Cup.

Neither of these grounds can in any way compete with the

two American stadiums in amenities or club activities, with the result that they often appear deserted. In addition, they are frequently hired out for activities which have nothing to do with Association football. Nowadays, admission to Wembley for the great matches it stages is by ticket only—a policy adopted after that eventful first Wembley final between Bolton Wanderers and West Ham United in 1923, to which reference has already been made.

Frequently, the location and condition of English football grounds are the consequence of their origin. Sometimes a ground has been constructed upon land owned by its founder and first chairman. Sometimes, again, the ground has been leased from the local authority. Others in the beginning were little more than patches of waste ground, roughly enclosed with wood or corrugated iron. In the early days of the Football League, two conditions were thought to be desirable. The first was that the ground should be situated as near as possible to the areas in which manual workers lived, for at this period Association football was almost the only winter sport which they could regularly watch. Since working men were proverbially tough, and the 6d (2½p) gate which survived until 1914 allowed for few improvements, there was little immediate demand for shelter. Even when the first stands were built, they were unpleasing structures of wood and iron, built with little regard for comfort, the roofs being supported by rows of pillars. When crowds increased and it became necessary to raise banking, this was done by the simple expedient of bringing in earth, rubble and cinders from neighbouring building sites and collieries, and cutting rough terraces in this material when it had settled. On many grounds, spectators were familiar with areas from which an unobstructed view of the playing pitch was impossible. When the crowds assembled at Crystal Palace for the Cup Final were in the neighbourhood of 100,000, it is doubtful whether half of those who paid for admission were able to see much of the match from the grassy slopes of the bowl in which the game was played.

The second requirement in the early days was that the ground should be not too far distant from a railway station. Otherwise, too much time would be consumed in reaching it. Accordingly, as the town grew, the ground gradually became increasingly hemmed in, leaving no room for expansion or, in later days, for car parks. One consequence of this is that journeys of any distance up to a mile may have to be traversed on foot from the place where the car is parked (usually a side-street) to the ground. This can be a substantial deterrent.

Removal to another ground can be a hazardous experiment. One which readily springs to mind, and which has already been mentioned, was the move of the Arsenal from Plumstead to Highbury. At a later date Charlton have found the south-east of London lethargic in its support—possibly because the attachment of dockland has always been to West Ham and Millwall. But it is easy to forget today that the first years of the Arsenal's tenure of Highbury continued the story of lukewarm support which began in Plumstead.

The moves of Manchester City from Fallowfield, and of Sheffield Wednesday from Olive Grove (now for many years railway sidings) to Hillsborough have proved to be very great successes, although in both cases the clubs appeared to be moving some distance from their firmest supporters. But it is not only the location of the ground, but also its size, which is of importance. Queen's Park Rangers have a small ground at Loftus Road, Shepherd's Bush, under the shadow of the White City stadium, the capacity of which is approximately 100,000. When the club briefly reached the First Division, there was much discussion of the possibility of playing at the White City. Two factors were principally responsible for the decision to stay at Loftus Road. The first, as the then-manager, Alec Stock, acutely pointed out, was that whilst the White City might be a good ground for a successful First Division club (as Stamford Bridge is for Chelsea), if the club was struggling, a small, and perhaps dispirited, crowd would be lost in its great spaces. The second factor was that the game would be played on a pitch unusually distant from the stands, and the players would miss the encouragement they derived from spectators who were so near the touchline that they could almost lean over and touch the players. When Luton descended in a few seasons from the First to the Fourth Division, plans for a new ground with a capacity of 50,000 and a fine car-park were indefinitely suspended.

It has already been mentioned that a number of leading clubs are spending a large part of the profits they earn on massive ground improvements. All have tightened up their safety precautions, and there is an annual safety survey at the beginning of each season. Having regard to the size of the crowds—exceeding a million—which assemble each week in England alone to watch football, the rarity of serious accidents is remarkable. In 1896, part of the stand of Blackburn Rovers collapsed with some injury to spectators. More recently, there was a similar accident at Burndon Park, the home of Bolton Wanderers, and the worst of all occurred at Ibrox Park, the home of Glasgow Rangers, at the end of a match early in 1971. The match was with their great rivals, Glasgow Celtic, watched by a capacity crowd of 80,000. Whilst the two earlier accidents could be attributed to faulty construction, the one at Ibrox Park depended upon factors so rare as to be virtually unforeseeable. Many spectators were already leaving the ground when, in the last minutes of play, the Rangers scored an equalising goal. The applause caused many of those leaving to attempt to return. One sharply descending staircase became hopelessly jammed. Many were trodden under foot, and others were pressed over the rails of the staircase.

The Ibrox Park tragedy had an important sequel. A Scottish judge, Lord Wheatley, was asked by the government to undertake an inquiry into the problem of safety at sports grounds, and in his report which appeared in May 1972,[1] Lord Wheatley says:

> My analysis of the existing arrangements has led me to the clear conclusion that they are not adequate. The system of certification introduced recently by the Football Association is defective in a number of respects.
>
> I do not consider it necessary to go into details on descriptions

---

[1] *Report of an Inquiry into Crowd Safety at Sports Grounds. Cmnd. 4952.*

of how inadequacies on football grounds can give rise to danger, injury or death. It is sufficient to say that the harm done can range from a minor injury to a major disaster.

Many of the stands used at present were built years ago. The materials of which they are built, their design, and the use to which the accommodation underneath is put may constitute fire risks.

People both inside and outside the football world are expecting something to be done now. In many quarters it has gone beyond expectancy to the point of demand.

The report therefore proposes that there should be a licensing system for sports grounds, which should be applicable to all except those with very small attendances. From the decision of the licensing authority, there will be an appeal to a special tribunal, comprising a legally-qualified chairman, an architect, surveyor or engineer, and a police officer with experience of crowd control.

The proposal to license sports grounds to which the public are invited is not new. It was made, but not followed up, in 1946, following the accident at Burnden Park, in which thirty-three people died after a crush barrier had given way. Under the present scheme, licensing will be introduced progressively, the grounds being divided into four categories:

1. International grounds, such as Hampden Park, Ninian Park, Wembley, Cardiff Arms Park, Murrayfield, and Twickenham, and, in addition, the grounds of English First and Second Division clubs and those of Scottish First Division clubs.

2. The grounds of English Third and Fourth Division clubs and Scottish Second Division clubs, and all Rugby League clubs.

3. The grounds of all other Soccer and Rugby clubs (whether Rugby League or Rugby Union) with a capacity of more than 10,000.

4. Grounds with a capacity of not more than 10,000, but which possess a stand.

The report has been accepted by the government as the basis for legislation, which will be the product of consultation between the Home Office, the local authorities and the football clubs. One major problem is that of finance, more especially for the smaller clubs. The question of a government subsidy or loan has already been raised, and so has the possibility of raising a special fund from all the clubs. One of the major difficulties is that the grounds which may need the greatest reconstruction may also belong to clubs which have quite insufficient resources to undertake it.

A constant modern menace is hooliganism on the part of a small section of the crowd, not only on the ground itself but also in the vicinity of it after a match. It is usually begun by the so-called supporters of the defeated club, and it is proving difficult to eradicate. So far as the ground is concerned, clubs have not yet resorted to the South American expedient of erecting iron grilles, or to the Italian method of building a moat and iron fence. Instead, a number of leading members of many supporters' clubs have undertaken the onerous task of crowd-marshals, and co-operation from this source is likely to be the most hopeful line of approach. It ought also to be mentioned that the control of crowds remains a matter for the club itself, which employs for the occasion what it considers to be an adequate number of police. Of course, if breaches of the peace or other crimes occur, it is the duty of the police to carry out their normal duties, and possibly one of the most striking features of these occasions is the good humour and imperturbability of the policemen themselves.

Nevertheless the question of crowd disorder is one which tends to bring a club into discredit, and those who govern football very properly treat it as one of the chief problems of modern football. In the past, the Football Association and the Football League have not hesitated to close for a period grounds on which serious disorder has occurred. Since 1945, the grounds of Plymouth, Gillingham and Millwall have all been closed for a short period. Possibly the most serious disturbance up to the present time occurred on 17 April 1971, when Leeds United received West Bromwich Albion. At that time, Leeds United and the Arsenal were in keen and close competition for the League Championship, and Leeds United ultimately lost this match by two goals to one, after the referee had allowed a goal scored by West Bromwich which the Leeds supporters claimed was offside. Members of the crowd rushed onto the pitch and attacked the referee and a linesman, the latter being injured by a missile. Eventually the police cleared the pitch, and restored order, but the episode was complicated, first by the attitude of the Leeds players, and secondly by statements made by the manager and chairman of Leeds United, suggesting that there was provocation for what had occurred, and also that the referee had erred. It was well-known that the episode was regarded with the greatest anxiety by all referees, and on 10 June a joint disciplinary committee ordered: (i) that the Leeds ground should be closed for three weeks from 14 August, (ii) that the Leeds club should compensate visiting teams for any loss of revenue arising from the closure, and (iii) that the manager and chairman of the club be severely censured. There can be no doubt that this irruption caused anxiety on the national scale, together with a good deal of press comment, and Mr Hardaker, the secretary of the Football League, and others responsible for the organisation of football, have emphasised that if unruly behaviour continues there will be no alternative but to take similar steps to those which have already been taken in Italy and South America. It may be simply one phase of the general indiscipline of the present age, but it nevertheless presents the most serious threat which Association football has yet faced. Nor is it open to question that numbers of people now stay away from matches because of the possibility of injury.

There can be no doubt that these ugly manifestations of collective hooliganism are being taken most seriously by the clubs, more especially since the closure of the Leeds ground was followed shortly afterwards by the closure for two weeks of the ground of Manchester United, for a mysterious incident in which a knife was thrown on the pitch near to the visiting goalkeeper, whilst a match was in progress. This, in turn, was followed by an outbreak of hooliganism by alleged supporters of Manchester United in the streets of Halifax before a match between Manchester and Halifax immediately prior to the opening of the League programme for 1971-72. Possibly the most significant step so far taken has been that of the Everton club in requiring supporters wishing to purchase tickets for away matches to sign a pledge of good behaviour before they are issued with tickets. The club is also taking measures to ensure good behaviour on trains and coaches carrying supporters. Both have suffered seriously from vandalism in the recent past.

Football crowds deserve closer study than they have yet received. Why are the supporters of Liverpool (a wealthy and successful First Division club) and those of Oldham Athletic (once a power in football, recently for a number of seasons condemned to the Fourth Division, but now happily promoted to the Third) renowned for their sportsmanship, whilst those of other clubs (which must be nameless) are the reverse? Has it anything to do with the behaviour of the players themselves, as has sometimes been suggested? It was at one time feared that the growth of football pools might be responsible in part for the deterioration in the behaviour of some parts of a crowd, but this theory has been abandoned, for it is abundantly evident that the irrational antics of young hooligans owe nothing to this source. It is, one perceives, only one aspect of the steady drift towards violence manifested increasingly in our urban society, and it is not possible to suggest an easy solution. One thing is, however, apparent. If magistrates impose only small fines for such offences, they will be regarded with contempt by these disturbers of the peace.

Something must be said of some of the best grounds in the country (including Scotland). A small group of these, selected for games in the World Cup Tournament in 1966, received substantial grants to improve their amenities. These were Goodison Park (home of Everton FC), Old Trafford (home of Manchester United FC), Hillsborough (home of Sheffield Wednesday FC), and Ayresome Park (home of Middlesbrough FC). These must therefore now rank high in any list, and to them should be added White Hart Lane (Tottenham Hotspur FC), Highbury (the Arsenal FC), St James' Park (Newcastle United FC), Maine Road (Manchester City FC), Anfield Road (Liverpool FC), Stamford Bridge (Chelsea FC), and Elland Road (Leeds United FC). All these grounds, it will be noticed, belong to clubs which have done exceptionally well in modern times, and three of them are London grounds. Potentially, one could add a fourth, Selhurst Park, where Crystal Palace, now in the First Division, and at last, by energetic management and direction, tasting prosperity, are undertaking far-reaching developments. Each of these grounds has a capacity in excess of 60,000, and upon occasion the full capacity is needed to accommodate those who wish to watch. In 1968, as has been noticed, Manchester United had an average home gate of 57,000, and Liverpool, Everton, Manchester City, Leeds United and Tottenham Hotspur were not far behind. Chelsea and the Arsenal now both enjoy gates of approximately 40,000, although in the keenness of competition between the London clubs and in the light of publicity from the London press, crowds will rapidly desert a less successful club for a neighbour which is enjoying a run of success.

In the inter-war years, Maine Road more than once housed a crowd exceeding 80,000, as did Highbury and Chelsea. In the same period, Goodison Park, Old Trafford, Anfield Road and Hillsborough admitted more than 70,000 for a Cup-tie. Safety, as has been stated, has compelled a reduction of these numbers, and today there is more seating accommodation on all these grounds, at substantially higher prices, to compensate for these reductions. Moreover, seating has become more comfortable than that—often no more than long planking—which was thought to be adequate in the stands built in an earlier era. If football is to have the general appeal it has in Latin America, the comfort of spectators must be a major preoccupation. In this respect, the football ground must compare not unfavourably with the local cinema.

For this reason in particular, the imaginative scheme of ground development which has been adopted by Chelsea FC deserves special mention. The Chelsea club owes very much to the enthusiasm of successive generations of the Mears family. It was founded by two brothers, H. A. and J. T. in 1905, the present ground at Stamford Bridge having been bought for £5,000 when it was used as a dumping ground for material excavated from the underground railway which was then under construction. When the founders were no longer there, J.T.'s son, familiarly known as 'Joe', took over and served as chairman for twenty-six years. The present chairman, Brian, has continued where his father left off. Now that Chelsea are among the most successful of the League clubs, he has been the inspiration for a scheme which could make Stamford Bridge the first stadium, outside Wembley, in the country. Estimated to cost over two million pounds, it will include new stands, a large and well-appointed restaurant, and the most modern gymnasium, dressing-rooms and equipment. This projected development is significant. Chelsea attracts a body of support which is a good deal wider than that of most clubs. It includes professional men, actors, artists and the colourful population of the King's Road. The amenities of the new stadium could make it a rallying point for them in something like the way the South American stadiums are.

If the balance sheets of professional clubs are examined, it will be found that catering either does not appear at all, or else is an astonishingly small item, yielding profits of no more than one or two thousand pounds a year. Here again, the English football clubs have been blinkered by their earlier history. Until very recently they have assumed that a pint of beer and a pie were all that was needed to supply their supporters with refreshment —and this throughout a long winter.

The entire question of catering is one which needs to be taken into consideration in schemes for the modernisation of the greater grounds, and it might well be that clubs would profit from consultations with some of the leading firms of caterers when major improvements are being considered. Those who promoted dog-racing in major stadiums were aware of the benefits of adequate facilities when designing them, and it should be recognised that social habits have changed to a remarkable degree since 1945. Dining-out at varying levels is now universal, and when both husband and wife are employed it is a much-needed relaxation. Further, the proportion of those who work on Saturday

F

morning has greatly diminished, so that a meal before a game would be within the reach of large numbers of potential spectators, who might be additionally attracted by the prospect of securing a good place in the car-park. Failure to make such provision ignores the fact that watching football is now comparable with a visit to the cinema, and every effort should be made to encourage the attendance of families, and not, as before, their adult male members only. It is this factor which gives South American football clubs their very great drawing power.

There are, however, other standards of comparison. The United States has many great arenas for American football and for baseball administered on commercial lines, and no effort has been spared to make them attractive. In a first-class ground, there is complete seating under cover and an unobstructed view from every seat. There is also a full service of refreshments, whether a full meal or simply food and drinks which may be consumed whilst the game is in progress. Normally, this service is operated by a catering firm which has bought the concession.

Baseball and American football have also exploited television rights to the full. Since television in the United States is wholly commercial, there is keen competition among programme sponsors. So far as the clubs are concerned, there may be disadvantages, but there are also benefits. It is certain that the availability of so much television coverage of baseball, coupled with lively commentaries, has brought a continuing decline in attendances. Twenty years ago New York had three major league baseball teams, well-known both nationally and internationally. Declining support, coupled with fantastic increases in the wages paid to players, necessitated the removal of the Dodgers and the Giants, and today the Dodgers have their home in California. It is awareness of this dismal possibility which is responsible for the cautious attitude which the Football Association and the Football League have always shown to television. For the professional clubs of Great Britain, television offers few compensating advantages. In the United States, where baseball clubs are expected to operate in accordance with general commercial practice, a baseball team may be a principal element in a combine of activities which, in turn, controls television time. The club, in such a complex, may be the principal attraction through which attention to the manufactured product may be directed, and it may therefore expect to draw money from the industry, so long as its power to boost sales is apparent. It is fortunate that professional football in England has not followed American practice in this respect. Nevertheless, there are some lessons to be learned.

There remains a further question for discussion. A number of the principal cities in the United Kingdom possess two clubs which operate in the Football League. The problems which this may create have already been mentioned, but it should also be noticed that it promotes a very keen rivalry from which supporters of both clubs within the city profit. The two-club cities are Liverpool (Everton and Liverpool), Manchester (United and City), Birmingham (City and Aston Villa), Sheffield (Wednesday and United), Nottingham (Forest and County), and Bristol (City and Rovers). London, Glasgow and Edinburgh all have more than two. There are also some other clubs which are very close neighbours—eg, Blackpool and Preston, Leeds and Huddersfield, and Stoke and Port Vale. Since a club regularly stages a first-team match only once a fortnight, it has sometimes been rather superficially suggested in the press that they might use a common ground, playing second and junior team matches on some lesser ground (which again might be shared). Such suggestions are attractive only to persons with little knowledge of local conditions, and even an elementary consideration shows them to be impracticable. What happens, for example, if both teams are drawn at home in an FA Cup-tie? What about arrears of fixtures in all competitions at the end of the season? How can the costs of development be apportioned assuming that support of the two clubs is unequal, as it will be if they are in different divisions? Even if these and allied difficulties are overcome, there remain other and deeper reasons against such a proposal. It would perhaps be an overstatement to say that football supporters are born supporting one club or the other; but loyalties,

even to grounds, run very deep and are written into the history
of football. The highly-successful Liverpool club, with its splen-
did facilities, was formed as a result of a profound split in the
Everton club, and one half of Liverpool is as attached to Anfield
Road as the other half is to Goodison Park. It is very difficult to
imagine Aston Villa playing regularly at St Andrews, and it is
virtually unbelievable that Birmingham would ever settle down
comfortably at Villa Park, where the traditions of a mighty past
still linger among a devoted band of supporters. And how could
any supporter of Huddersfield Town, whatever their fortunes
may be, ever forget that once the fortunes of the club were
at such a low ebb that they almost moved lock, stock and barrel
from Leeds Road, Huddersfield, into Leeds itself, to be saved at
the last moment by the devotion of a chairman and one of those
football miracles which, against all the odds, *do* occur from time
to time? In the last resort, possession of a ground (even if it is
only rented from the council) is the ultimate guarantee of the
continued existence and independence of the club.

One final word should be added on the question of rates.
These, as the club balance sheets show, can be a very heavy burden; but there are special principles which must be applied. In
Tomlinson v. *Plymouth Argyle FC*[1] the club appealed against a
decision of the Lands Tribunal, assessing its ground and
premises at £2,250 rateable value. The Court of Appeal set aside
the decision of the Lands Tribunal, directing them to reconsider
the value, and, in doing so, to decide on the basis that the club
was the only possible tenant, and to take into consideration the
history and finances of the club.

---

[1] (1960) 53 R. & I.T. 297.

5
Some Football Casualties

Is there anything to be learned from an analysis of some of football's casualties? Their histories are by no means always accounts of failure, nor are major casualties confined to professional football. Some failures were once outstandingly successful clubs, which have in their day attracted many famous players, and a good deal of support. Further, the list of casualties includes the names of some of the most famous amateur clubs, although it is the list of those clubs which attained League status and failed to maintain it which is of the greatest general interest.

Modern football owes more than can be briefly stated to the pioneering activities of the Wanderers, in the days before the Football League, or even the FA Cup competition, existed. The club attracted outstanding amateur players from all sides, and some of them, such as C. W. Alcock and Lord Kinnaird, served for many years on the committees of the Football Association in its earliest, and most difficult years. In the first Cup competition, in 1872, the Wanderers drew with Queen's Park, their famous Scottish counterparts. The match was played in London, and since the Scots were unable to finance a prolonged stay, they returned to Glasgow, leaving the Wanderers to go forward to win the first Cup Final before a crowd of 2,000 spectators, defeating the Royal Engineers by the only goal of the match. The following year when, under the Cup rules which then prevailed, they were exempted until the Final, once again they were the victors, defeating Oxford University by two clear goals. A year or two later, they won the Cup in three successive years—an achievement which, in all probability, will never be equalled. Again, under the rules, they had won the Cup outright, but they returned it to the Association for competition, on condition that it should never become the property of any club.

During the 'seventies the Wanderers, with a number of Old Boys' clubs, the Royal Engineers and Oxford University monopolised the semi-final and final ties, but as the 'eighties opened, their names appear at this stage less frequently, and by the end of the decade had disappeared. There were a number of reasons. The great figures whose robust style had set the pattern for the game in its first phase had grown older and had substituted the administration of football for participation in it. But new names of city clubs, with players trained to a greater degree of fitness than the members of the first clubs, were appearing, and when Blackburn Olympic beat the Old Etonians at the Oval in 1883, having also accounted for the Old Carthusians in the semi-final, the domination of the Cup competition by the great southern amateur clubs was over. The Wanderers were to continue for some years longer without establishing a place in the new structure of football. They never had the inclination, as their great Scottish rivals, Queen's Park, had, to enter the Football League, and accordingly they passed into history, giving place to a newer amateur club, the Corinthians.

The Corinthians were formed in 1884 at the moment when the drift towards professionalism had become unmistakable, but although they were able to hold their own with the best of the professional sides, and were able to field a number of internationals, they were debarred by their rules from competing for the FA Cup. In 1885 and 1886, Blackburn Rovers won the Cup, but in both seasons they were defeated by the Corinthians by a wide margin. There is little doubt that, had they entered for the Cup during their great years, they would have proved winners on more than one occasion, more especially since in 1889 they defeated by five clear goals Preston North End, who had just achieved the 'double' by winning both the League and the Cup.

Long after, when the name of the Corinthians had lost much of its magic, they entered regularly for the Cup, and largely as a concession to their former greatness, they were regularly granted exemption until the first or (when the competition was reorganised to take in the Third, and later the Fourth Division) the third round. Even so, this did little more than secure them a single game. Since they had not competed regularly in any competition before the game, and since there were uncertainties about the composition of the side, it was not to be expected that they could defeat professional sides. When their special exemption ceased there was no longer any point in entering the Cup competition, and eventually they declined to such a point that it was necessary for them to merge with another club, drawing its players from former University men—the Casuals. Somewhat ingloriously, they still survive in this form in the Isthmian League, and still compete in the Amateur Cup, not very successfully.

Still another famous amateur organisation enjoyed a brief life after 1945. A group of Oxford and Cambridge players, organised by Dr Thompson (now a member of the FA Council), formed the Pegasus FC, with the object of contributing to the development of amateur football. They, too, were given special exemption in the FA Cup competition, but once again their achievements fell somewhat short of expectation, for the same reason that those of the Corinthians had done in the earlier period, and Pegasus is now no more.

It will be generally agreed that the success of a really powerful amateur club would be good for the game as a whole, more especially as in recent years some well-known and successful amateur clubs have turned professional. Could the history of those three famous amateur clubs have been a longer one? It is possible to answer this question by comparing them with Queen's Park in Scotland. Founded in 1867 at the same time as the Wanderers, they competed regularly in the early Cup tournaments, and were unlucky not to win it on several occasions. Between 1874 and 1893, they won the Scottish Cup nine times. Having bought a ground at Hampden Park for £10,000 in 1899, they entered the Scottish League in 1900, and have remained there ever since, even though today they remain in the Second Division. The days of their great battles with Rangers and Celtic are gone, but since international matches and Cup Finals are played at Hampden Park—probably the most impressive ground in the British Isles—they are free from financial difficulties. The club's abiding problem is the steady loss of their most promising young players to professional clubs. But for this, there would be no reason to suppose that Queen's Park could not return to their former greatness. Nevertheless, the services which they have performed in keeping amateur football alive in Scotland probably exceed in value that of the three English clubs together. Upon numerous occasions, the entire Scottish amateur international team has been composed of players from Queen's Park. Their survival, as contrasted with the disappearance of the three English amateur clubs, may be attributed to the fact that they have a permanent headquarters, managed by a committee who are mainly ex-players, and that competition in the Scottish League, difficult as it now is, has given the amateurs a continuing standard of play as well as a major objective. This is a test to which no English amateur club has submitted itself, although there is nothing to prevent one from applying to join the League. For a brief time in the inter-war period there was a suggestion that there should be such a club, the Argonauts, but it was not pursued.

Beside these illustrious names, those of the professional clubs which were at one time members of the Football League but failed to maintain their place may perhaps lack familiarity, but their histories do not lack significance. First, it should be mentioned that some clubs which lost their League status have been able to regain it when the League has been extended. There are a number of others which have been less fortunate. Of these, the most important is possibly Accrington Stanley, one of the very few clubs to resign from the League during the playing season. This they did on March 6, 1962, and their failure was Oxford United's opportunity. Not only were they founder-members of the Football League, but they had been entering for the FA Cup some years earlier, and in 1883 they were temporarily expelled from membership of the FA for playing men who were declared to be professionals. Increasing expenses compelled them to withdraw from the League in 1895, and they were therefore one of the clubs which recovered League status by joining the Third Division (North) on its foundation in 1921. At the end of the 1959-60 season, they were relegated to the Fourth Division, having gained only 27 points, but they completed only one season there, not very successfully. By this time, support had dwindled to 2-3,000 a match, and the club was heavily in debt. These difficulties are not peculiar to Accrington, and the club had survived the long-drawn-out depression of the 'thirties. Wherein lay the difference? Part of it, perhaps, may be found in the *AA Handbook*. Accrington has a population of only 36,810, which is considerably below the comfortable level for the support of a League club. The town is only six miles from Burnley, and only five from Blackburn. It is sixteen miles from Bolton, thirteen from Bury, fifteen from Preston, fifteen from Rochdale and, finally, only twenty-one from Manchester. Surrounded by no less than seven League clubs, most of them with extremely distinguished records, the miracle is that Accrington survived so long.

When the Third Section (Northern) was founded just after the first war, its original membership included an unduly high proportion of Lancashire clubs. This was primarily because the Lancashire towns of the second rank have, in the past, developed a number of really good clubs. Unfortunately one or two besides Accrington have failed to survive. Nelson and Wigan Borough were both original members of this section. Nelson finished at the bottom at the end of the season 1930-31 with only 19 points. Wigan started the 1931-32 season, but financial difficulties compelled them to resign in October 1931. Today they apply regularly for admission to the Fourth Division, but they have not so far been re-admitted in spite of an impressive record in Cup-ties in recent years. Once again the *AA Handbook* may supply a reason. Nelson is only four miles from Burnley, and even today its population is no more than 31,400. Wigan is substantially larger—its population is 79,410, and there is no very close competition. Blackburn, Liverpool, Manchester and Southport are all twenty miles away, and Preston is seventeen miles. For Lancashire—packed with football clubs as it is—these are comfortable distances, but Wigan, and several neighbouring towns, are also centres of Rugby League football. The chief reason for the failures of Nelson and Wigan however was the depression of the 'thirties, which paralysed the cotton industry. Once again, there are problems in Lancashire soccer today. At the end of 1970-71 season, Burnley and Blackpool descended to Division II, and Blackburn Rovers, with Bolton Wanderers, dropped to the Third. For clubs with such great achievements in the past, this is a sharp reminder of present-day competition in the League which may strike down the very greatest—as Preston North End and Aston Villa had discovered at the end of the previous season.

Blackburn Rovers might have had competition even nearer home, for the first Blackburn club to achieve success was not the Rovers, but Blackburn Olympic in 1883. They were the first club to take the Cup from the southern amateur clubs. Their exploit was quickly overshadowed by the success of their neighbours, Blackburn Rovers, in the following season, and thereafter, whilst the Rovers were winning the Cup five times in eight years, Blackburn Olympic gradually faded from view. When the League was formed, it was the Rovers who became one of the first twelve, and without League football there could be no assurance of regular support.

The list of those professional clubs which, although once members of the Football League, have failed to preserve their League status, is a surprisingly short one. Besides the three Lancashire clubs already mentioned, it comprises Aberdare Athletic, Ashington, Bootle, Bradford, Burton Swifts, Burton Wanderers, Darwen, Gainsborough Trinity, Glossop, Loughborough Town, New Brighton Tower, Northwich Victoria, South Shields (Gateshead), Walsall Town Swifts, and Thames.

Of these, Darwen and Glossop belong to the early history of football. At that time Darwen was a most lively centre, for besides the club which eventually entered the League, two others, Lower Darwen and Darwen Ramblers, entered for the

FA Cup, and in Blackburn Olympic's progress to the Final in 1882-83, they defeated these two clubs in successive games. The Darwen club itself reached the fourth round as early as 1878-79, and they were one of the first clubs to adopt the disguised part-time professionalism which was ultimately accepted by the Football Association. For all their Cup-fighting exploits, their League career was short. They were one of the original members of the Second Division, but withdrew in 1899, having accumulated the meagre total of nine points out of thirty League games. Glossop's League career was a good deal longer. They were admitted to the Second Division in 1898, and remained in membership until the outbreak of the War of 1914-18. By the end of it, the club had virtually ceased to exist, and not only did they not rejoin the Second Division, they did not reappear when the Northern Section of the Third Division was formed. Neither Glossop nor Darwen are towns with populations big enough to support League football. Today, that of Glossop is approximately 20,000 and that of Darwen is between 28,000 and 30,000. To this should be added the comment that Darwen is four miles from Blackburn and nine from Bolton.

At the end of the season 1969-70, Bradford (Park Avenue) failed to be re-elected to the Fourth Division. For three successive seasons they had finished at the bottom. This was a lamentable decline for a club which had once won the Cup and had been briefly in the First Division. The greatest days of Bradford football were in the years between 1900 and 1914. During that time, both Bradford teams won the Cup, Bradford City reached the First Division of the League in 1908 and Bradford in 1914. The inter-war years were disastrous, and one club followed the other into the Northern Section, and when the Fourth Division was formed, both Bradford clubs descended to it. When Bradford City gained promotion from the Fourth to the Third in 1969 it was the first time a Bradford club had won promotion since 1914—even though in between they had played occasionally with success in the Cup. For many years it had been strongly urged that Bradford could support only one professional Association football club, more especially as the city also supports a strong professional Rugby League club.

Of two other clubs, very little need be said. Neither Bootle nor New Brighton could hope to survive indefinitely as a League club in view of the success and drawing power of the two Liverpool clubs. This has also affected Tranmere Rovers, once a successful Second Division club, with the habit of discovering famous centreforwards. Of these, the one who is best known is 'Dixie' Dean. New Brighton (originally New Brighton Tower) was another of those clubs which, after a brief spell of three seasons in the Second Division at the turn of the century, returned to League football with the extension of the Northern section in 1923.

Two other clubs, which in very different ways failed to establish themselves against famous local rivals, were Thames and South Shields (or Gateshead). The League career of Thames extended only over the seasons 1930-31 and 1931-32. At the end of the second season, they finished at the bottom of the Southern Section and withdrew. They owed their election primarily to the fact that the depression of the 'thirties had brought about the withdrawal of several clubs. Thames was a synthetic club. It played at West Ham stadium, and had no local roots.

The history of South Shields is quite different. Tyneside has produced many famous players, and local support for Association football has always been very strong. South Shields itself has a population of over 100,000, and there are other smaller towns close at hand. Nevertheless, after their decline to the Northern Section, South Shields failed to attract substantial support, and in 1930 they moved to Gateshead, where they survived precariously until the reorganisation of the Third Division (North) and the Third Division (South). They descended to the Fourth Division, and after two seasons withdrew. The club had always found the counter-attraction of its two great neighbours, Newcastle United and Sunderland, too great to combat effectively, and at no time in its League history had it been able to do anything to capture increased local support.

Aberdare Athletic had six seasons in the Third Division (South) between 1921 and 1927. Their decline may be traced directly to the decline of the Welsh mining industry after the first world war. Ashington's career in the Third (North) was a little longer—from 1921 to 1928—but its failure can be traced to a similar cause, for Ashington is also a colliery town, this time on the Durham coalfield.

There remains a group of Midlands clubs. One of them merits only a single comment. Walsall Town Swifts played in the Second Division for the first three years of its existence. They are therefore the predecessors of the present Walsall club, which was elected to the Second Division in 1896. In spite of its nearness to Birmingham and Wolverhampton, the club has managed to maintain its League status, and has sometimes captured popular enthusiasm by outstanding successes in the Cup competition.

At various times, two clubs represented Burton in the Second Division of the League—the Swifts (later Burton United) and the Wanderers. The Swifts joined the Second Division at its foundation, and remained in continuous membership until 1907. The Wanderers lasted for three seasons only, from 1894 until 1897. Neither team made any effort to rejoin on the formation of either section of the Third Division, although Burton, with a population of over 50,000, is not unfavourably placed. Today, still another Burton club, Burton Albion, competes as a professional club in the Southern League. Northwich Victoria lasted only the first two seasons after the formation of the Second Division, and on the second occasion gained only nine points. With a population of less than 20,000, the effort was too great for them. Loughborough Town competed in the Second Division for five seasons between 1895 and 1900. They fought a losing battle, which was emphasised by the success of Leicester in the same division. The original club had been dissolved, but another had been formed in its place when the two sections of the Third Division were being formed, but it made no effort to join the League. Gainsborough Trinity were a Second Division club from 1896 to 1912, usually in the lower half of the final table. Once again the effort was too great for a town which today has a population of no more than 18,000. On the whole, Lincolnshire is not a stronghold of professional football, as the present lowly position of Lincoln City, Grimsby and Scunthorpe show.

This brief survey of the fortunes of those clubs which did not preserve their League membership reveals a few interesting points. If the fleeting membership of Thames is ignored, the South has suffered no permanent losses, although Gillingham once retired, but returned with the Southern Section. Wales has suffered one loss and the North-East two, in areas where there were few League clubs. The greatest losses have been in Lancashire, where the early enthusiasm for professional football produced clubs which were situated too close together. In spite (or perhaps because) of the great achievements of the two Manchester clubs and the two Liverpool clubs since the war, the position of the other Lancashire clubs is weakening progressively. The losses in the Midlands have been in part due to the dominance of the Birmingham clubs, Stoke, Leicester and Derby County. As in Lancashire, football in the Midlands was organised early, and it produced a great deal of enthusiasm, and a number of clubs which have failed to stay the course. The South, which turned to professionalism later than the rest of the country, has gained steadily at the expense of the Midlands and Lancashire. This, however, is far from being the full story. The pattern of industry has changed, and there has been a steady drift of population in its wake to the South. If this continues, the balance must swing still further in favour of the South.

One other factor may be mentioned. In Yorkshire and Lancashire, Association football shares popular support with Rugby League football, which is also professional. There is no comparable competition in the South, for although many of the great Rugby Union clubs have their headquarters there, it is only for occasional matches that they attract any considerable following. Finally, in the inter-war period, a number of the country's leading amateur soccer clubs, situated in or around

London, attracted crowds numbering several thousands, which might grow to ten or twenty thousand in the semi-finals of the Amateur Cup. Today this is no longer the case—and the decline of amateur football is a matter which will be discussed in the next chapter.

6

The Amateur Game

By common consent, amateur football, although still played by thousands every week, is today in a precarious condition. For a brief period after the war of 1939-45 it flourished, and once or twice the Amateur Cup Final was played at Wembley before crowds of 60-80,000. Today only a few thousands, mainly from the areas from which the finalists are drawn, bother to attend. There is very little prior comment in the press, and the final game itself is briefly noticed. Amateur internationals attract even fewer spectators, and even less publicity. A dozen years ago, prominent amateur clubs, mainly in the Isthmian League, could attract attendances of four or five thousand. Today they have shrunk to a quarter or less. Some leading amateur clubs have disappeared completely from the scene. One or two others have become minor professional clubs. Something more will be said on this later, but it may be stated without fear of contradiction that amateur football has declined and is still declining. To this may be added the fact that today the odds seem to be heavily against amateur football.

Before proceeding further, it is necessary to attempt to resolve some of the confusion which envelops the classification of football players. There are today professionals, amateurs, permit players, apprentices, associated schoolboys, and service players—to which should perhaps be added true-blue amateurs who play for old boys' clubs and similar organisations, who still pay their own expenses, and enter only their own competitions. These are members of the Amateur Football Association, and they are the inheritors of the tradition which sought to prevent the introduction of professionalism ninety years ago.

The deep division of opinion over the recognition of professionalism which almost produced a split between the amateurs and professionals (such as actually occurred in Rugby football) was removed by a compromise which legalised professionalism, but which left the professional in a subordinate position. Today, the marks of inferior status are steadily disappearing. Notably, as has been stated, former professional players may now serve on the Football Association and on the boards and committees of football clubs, but some irritating restrictions remain, mostly in connection with 'permit' players.

Amateur status today is a brittle one, and may be easily lost. Rule 24 of the Football Association says, rather bleakly, that 'when a player is registered as a professional, he at once loses his status as an amateur', but the rule goes a good deal further. It declares that any player (other than an apprentice) who receives any payment or gift beyond permitted expenses (and these may include money prizes in football contests or in competitions run as an adjunct thereto in which even participation without winning is penalised) may also be declared (ie, by the competent authority) a professional. Today, of course, this could only occur after a properly-conducted hearing.

Amateur status is protected by Rule 25, a lengthy and discursive rule which is intended to establish a code of conduct and to prohibit all illegal payments. If an amateur is paid by the club for which he is registered in any other capacity, eg, as coach or groundsman, this must be immediately reported to the Football Association. If an amateur receives any payment at all, he must give a receipt which gives particulars of the expenses incurred. A standard form for expenses exists and must be used, and the rule is emphatic that extravagant or unnecessary expenses must not be paid. Further, a club or any one on its behalf who offers, directly or indirectly, an inducement to an amateur player to transfer from one club to another is guilty of misconduct.

The expenses which may be paid legitimately are set out in the rule in detail. The most important point in respect of them is that they cannot include lost wages, except in one instance— when a player attends trial matches or coaching sessions with a

G

professional club with a view to being registered as a professional.

The detail which is included in this rule reflects the continuing anxiety of the Football Association to preserve amateur status, and from time to time some amateur club falls foul of the rule. Then there is an investigation, and there are penalties. Unfortunately, such investigations scarcely touch the fringe of the problem, and they leave the world of football with the impression that the club has been either unlucky or has persistent enemies. No-one with any experience of modern senior amateur football can deny that substantial payments are made to the players of many senior amateur clubs—the principal exception being old boys' clubs, members of banks' clubs, and similar organisations which do not generally draw on outside players. Most attempts to stop the payment of regular sums (sometimes described as 'boot money') have foundered on the conspiracy of silence which envelops these transactions. Naturally such payments do not appear on the books of football clubs. They are buried in the accounts of supporters' clubs, or they may even go entirely unrecorded. One circumstance in connection with such payments is rarely mentioned. Being a secret transaction, no part of the 'expense' bears income-tax. As yet, the Football Association has not finally abandoned the struggle. As recently as June 1971, the Council resolved that all amateurs taking part in the FA Cup, the Amateur Cup, or international or representative matches will have to sign written and witnessed declarations that they have not received payments for expenses in excess of those permitted under the rules which have been summarised above.

'Shamateurism' in football has often been attacked, and there can be little doubt that public awareness of it has been a contributory factor in the decline of support for amateur clubs, not only on the touchline but also in the committee room. A person of standing is apt to think twice before becoming responsible for the activities of a club in which such payments are made. Even if they are so carefully concealed that he himself cannot be directly linked with them, it cannot fail to affect policy on the acquisition of players.

It will be observed that 'expenses' for amateur players are now in the curious half-light which enveloped the advent of professionalism in the nineteenth century. Definition can do little or nothing more to give precision to the distinction between professional and amateur status. It is evident that when a rule is generally disliked, it cannot be effectively enforced. Accordingly, the question may be asked: what is the value of preserving the distinction between amateur and professional footballers? Why should the Football Association and the county associations have the distasteful task of investigating accusations for irregular payments—often upon the most inadequate evidence?

It has been shown that in the past the distinction was largely a class distinction. The amateur had private means, and therefore the question of payment did not arise. That distinction has completely disappeared. Today, the great bulk of amateur players are ordinary working men and youths, and, if they are good enough, they hope to become professionals and to secure the great rewards which are now possible. In order to do this they are prepared to take their football very seriously, to train hard, and to suffer considerable inconvenience—but they expect to receive at least some compensation for the loss of leisure which it involves.

Professional clubs are rarely concerned with the problems of amateur players, but they are not indifferent to the continued existence of amateur football, for it is a recruiting-ground from which they may pick up a promising player without paying a transfer fee. It is here that problems would require solution if the distinction between the two sorts of player was abolished. There is no system of transfer fees between amateur clubs and, theoretically, no inducement may be offered to an amateur player to change his club. All the rules which at present protect the amateur player's freedom of choice would therefore need revision. Again, would the change apply to all players, or only to those who possess that mysterious thing, senior status?

It may be that the distinction must remain after all, and the Association is acting wisely in turning a blind eye to the fact that excessive expenses, sometimes exceeding the sums paid as wages to part-time professionals in non-League clubs, are regularly paid. This is one of the reasons why some amateur clubs have, in recent years, 'turned professional'. What this implies is simply that one or more players have been so registered. The club may still include amateurs and usually does so.

To suggest that clubs and players cling to their amateur status because it permits them to enter into major amateur competitions —such as the FA Amateur Cup or County Cup competitions— or even that it gives players a chance to represent their county in international games is quite unconvincing. A good young player today hopes to attract the attention of a professional club. Appearing in representative games certainly increases his chances, but today scouting systems are so extensive that there is little chance that a really good youth will pass unnoticed. So far as clubs are concerned, support for cup-ties, whether county or national, has dwindled like support for league matches. Only if an amateur club reaches the semi-final of the Amateur Cup can the club today expect to receive more than it has paid out in expenses.

Amateur players themselves are divided for playing purposes into senior and junior players. A senior player is one who has taken part for several seasons in his county senior cup competitions and, if the club for which he is a player is a senior club admitted to them, in the FA Cup and Amateur Cup competitions. Senior players usually play for senior clubs, but they may elect to play for junior clubs, and if they do they are debarred from taking part in junior cup competitions for a number of seasons.

A 'permit' player is one who has played as a professional but who wishes to continue playing without remuneration. For the most part, they are players who have signed professional forms at an early age, but who have failed to develop sufficiently to be retained. For many years such a player suffered many disabilities. He was debarred from playing for his club in county or national amateur competitions, he could not be a member of the committee of his league, or county association, or of the Football Association, and some amateur leagues refused to allow member clubs to play 'permit' players. Some of these disabilities have gone, but a number still remain, and are set out in Rule 30 of the Rules of the Football Association. There seems today no satisfactory reason for retaining them. The practice of the MCC in respect of former professionals is worthy of imitation here.

Service players, whilst serving, are under the jurisdiction of the football association of their service. Whether they have taken amateur or professional players before joining the service, they rank as amateurs so long as they are serving, and no club or person may attempt to induce any member of any of the services to play for an outside club, without giving at least fourteen days' written notice to the appropriate official in the service.

The position of apprentices is governed by Rule 32, and that of associated schoolboys by Rule 33. A player between the ages of fifteen and seventeen, who is not attached to a school, may be registered with the Football Association as a player for a professional club. Such clubs, of course, are mostly members of the Football League (with which the apprentice must also be registered if the registration is for a League club) but some non-League professional clubs occasionally also make use of this system. The number of apprentices registered by a club is limited to one for each five full-time professional players. On or after the apprentice's seventeenth birthday, he may sign as a professional for the club to which he has been attached, and the apprentice *must* make a decision whether or not to sign professional forms by his eighteenth birthday. If he does not sign, he reverts to full amateur status. That is to say, he is not condemned to live in the twilight of the 'permit'. All large League clubs now have elaborate training programmes for apprentices, and these may include provision for them to continue education or to undertake suitable vocational training.

The search for talented young players has now developed to the stage where schoolboys, especially schoolboy international players, are eagerly pursued. Rule 33 therefore provides that a schoolboy over thirteen may be registered by a Football League club or, under certain conditions, a non-League professional club, for purposes of coaching and training, but he may not play for his club until he reaches the school-leaving age, unless his headmaster agrees that he may do so. Once associated, the schoolboy may not change his club without the consent both of his original club and the headmaster. Since a league club may have attached to it up to forty schoolboys, it will be apparent that this vitally affects the recruitment of young players by amateur clubs.

Before discussing the amateur club further, it is well to remember that there is no hard-and-fast division between amateur and professional clubs. In the past, many leading professional clubs have regularly included amateurs—often very distinguished amateurs—in the teams which they have selected. If they are seen less frequently nowadays it is because even the gifted university amateur has to think of earning a living as soon as he leaves his university. In addition, the training schemes of leading clubs are so far developed that they now catch many young players who would frequently have escaped notice in the past. Finally, it may be pointed out that the rewards of the professional player are now so attractive that university graduates do not hesitate to become professionals.

At the other end of the scale there are clubs, sometimes in quite small towns, which employ no more than one or two professionals—perhaps on a part-time basis. Their presence may be expected to have a beneficial effect on the club's standard of play, and the main result of employing them is that the club is excluded from all purely amateur competitions, and also from the diminishing number of senior leagues which accept only clubs with amateur players. Since these amateur competitions today rarely attract a considerable gate, the exclusion can be borne with equanimity.

For a purely amateur club, other than one which is a member of a leading amateur league, entry for the FA Cup and the Amateur Cup has become almost a formalised ritual, in which one or perhaps two rounds are survived early in the season, and in each case the opponent was a local rival whom one usually meets in these competitions annually. If more rounds are survived, league fixtures become congested and will have to be played off at the end of the season, and county cup games accumulate. For this reason, the recent extensions of the playing season have been gratefully accepted by amateur clubs.

Amateur football clubs are rarely incorporated. They are members' clubs, with an annually elected committee and a secretary who is the channel of communication with the county association, the Football Association, and any leagues and competitions to which the club may be affiliated. In theory, the club committee is supported by a vigorous membership, broadly drawn from the area in which the club operates. All too often interest is tepid, membership is small, and even committee places may be hard to fill. Today, a disturbingly large number of senior amateur clubs continue to operate only because two or three enthusiasts are resolved to keep the flag flying. Each year, the expenses of running the club increase, and waning attendances have made contributions from supporters' clubs essential to the continuance of the club.

Although football enthusiasts rarely think of such things, the legal responsibilities of committee members are worthy of consideration. These are governed by the general law relating to unincorporated associations, and in particular, the rules relating to members' clubs. Much of it does not need to be explored in detail. No-one today, for example, is likely to bring legal proceedings to vindicate a right to membership, but it is well to remember the rules relating to liability. In *Brown* v. *Lewis*,[1] a case decided by the Divisional Court of the Queen's Bench Division in 1896, a spectator brought an action against Blackburn Rovers Football Club (which at that date had not yet become a limited liability company) for injuries suffered when the stand collapsed. The action was originally brought against two members of the committee, as representing the whole club, but the claim was amended, and the county court judge, finding that the stand had been negligently repaired, gave judgment against the mem-

---

[1] (1896) 12 T.L.R. 455.

bers of the committee personally for £25. In the Divisional Court this decision was upheld, and the judges emphasised that the committee were the persons primarily liable. 'They had the power and duty of providing a stand for the accommodation of the visitors to the football ground. They employed an incompetent man to repair the stand, and an accident resulted. The persons to blame were the committee.'

Possibly this decision had something to do with the progressive movement towards the incorporation of professional clubs. In any event, it has an important bearing on the operation of amateur clubs, whose committees would do well to insure against this form of liability. Equally, it should be pointed out that if the committee enters into contracts, it is they who are primarily liable upon them. These responsibilities in law are quite distinct from their obligations to leagues and associations to which they are affiliated, for here again they are the persons primarily responsible for any failure to fulfil obligations.

7
The Controlling Organisations

The organisation of Association football is one of great complexity. It is in fact a triumph of human ingenuity, albeit the result is a cumbrous structure which, like the British Constitution, almost defies explanation, must be experienced rather than understood, but which nevertheless works. Perhaps the most positive feature of modern football is the vast amount of time and skill which is cheerfully given, almost entirely without reward, to the organisation and development of the game. The very complexity of the organisation is in part the consequence of its comprehensiveness and in part the consequence of the history of the game. Of equal importance is the fact that, from the first, the Football Association has aimed to be an organisation founded on representative democracy. Thirdly, if at times the Association has appeared to move hesitantly, that is because its aim has always been to avert breakaways. It has therefore been prepared to compromise, sometimes at the expense of logic. Its attitude to the introduction of professionalism is an early example of this. Its present attitude towards the payment of excessive sums to amateurs in the guise of 'expenses' is another. After revising the rule which governs the payment of expenses, so that what is permissible is set out in considerable detail, and after a sporadic burst of activity by some county associations, the Football Association has now apparently allowed the whole matter to lapse. It is not yet prepared to abolish the distinction between amateurs and professionals altogether, so that all are simply players. On the other hand, it has made a first cautious move towards the control of amateur players by providing that an amateur may only transfer once from one club to another during a playing season, and also by providing with some exceptions that an amateur should not live too far away from the headquarters of the club for which he plays. Some years ago, the frequent transfers of leading amateur players from one club to another, and the fact that some of them were transported (sometimes even by air) long distances from distant homes, was unambiguous testimony to the inducements which were being offered. Today, this has been greatly reduced, although this may be due as much to the shrinkage of resources in supporters' clubs as to FA legislation.

The Association's greatest achievement has been the adoption of a uniform set of Laws of the Game which, with minor modifications, have served the game well ever since they were adopted. They are easy to understand, and they have produced a game which continues to attract large crowds wherever it is played skilfully, and it has proved as popular abroad as it has done in the British Isles. Another achievement in which it may legitimately take pride was the introduction of the open competition for the FA Cup which year by year arouses increasing enthusiasm as it progresses. There are other competitions, played on a home and away basis, but they do not compare with the FA Cup and its firm attachment to the knock-out principle, and its annual upsets of 'form'. Today, in addition to the FA Cup itself, the Association organises a similar competition for the Amateur Cup (now unfortunately losing its hold on public interest), another for professional non-league clubs, and one for youth teams. All of them are on a national basis. Although the bulk of the work of arranging fixtures has been delegated to other bodies, the Association itself has a full programme, for it arranges international matches (full, and amateur, and under-23), not only with the 'home' associations, but abroad; it has an imposing list of foreign tours, and another knock-out competition for amateurs organised by counties.

From the legal point of view, the Association is a limited company, incorporated on 13 June 1903 as a non-profitmaking organisation with a capital of £100, divided into 2,000 shilling (5p) shares. Presumably this change in structure was to enable it to own and handle its growing assets more easily. The signatories to the Memorandum of Association all played a most distinguished part in the development of the game, and they illustrate its comprehensive appeal. They were Lord Kinnaird; Charles Crump, described as 'Divisional Chief Clerk, Locomotive and Carriage Department, Great Western Railway', of Wolverhampton, but a celebrated player in his time and an FA Councillor for forty years; Sir Charles Clegg (not then knighted); the great C. W. Alcock; G. S. Sherrington (like Sir Charles Clegg, a solicitor); and finally Charles Hughes, described as 'Auctioneer and Valuer'.

Shares are allotted to members of the Council, to member clubs and to affiliated organisations, and a special block of eight has always been appropriated to the members of the committee of management of the Football League. This is a provision of the greatest importance, for the presence of these representatives of the League, with the power of the League behind them, has given very great weight to the League's views and on many occasions has restrained the activities of representatives of the county associations. Whenever a person ceases to be a member of the Council, or a representative of an association, or is excluded by the Council from membership, the share which he held is transferred or surrendered.

The Council of the Association is a large body, comprising between seventy and eighty members, and reflecting both the history and the federal structure of the Association. It includes the representatives of the county associations, of the services associations, of the Amateur Football Alliance (which once nearly broke away over the question of payment to amateurs), of the universities, of the public schools, and of the English Schools' Football Association. In addition, member clubs of the FA are divided into ten divisions, each of which elects a representative to the Council. Usually, an association is represented by its secretary, but representation is for the county association or other affiliated body to decide. Originally, most secretaries of county associations were paid only their expenses, but their work has in most cases grown to such proportions that the job is now frequently a full-time one. Whether, in these circumstances, the secretary remains the best representative of the county association is a matter which only the county itself can settle. Apart from this, there is at least one anomaly in the structure of the Association's Council. Although the Football League has always possessed eight representatives, there is no other direct representation from other leagues. These in their turn are divided into leagues which are 'sanctioned' by counties, and leagues 'sanctioned' directly by the FA, and these latter extend over three or more counties. Their numbers are not large, and it seems strange that they should be omitted.

Anyone who is familiar with the working of the Football Association is aware that, at times, there is a discernible difference in outlook between the representatives of the Football League and the rest. Occasionally it has become so serious that there have been suggestions that the League should break away completely, and become the responsible authority for professional football. It has not done so, partly because of a sense of loyalty to the parent body, partly because of an almost complete lack of interest in the fortunes of those lesser professional clubs which are outside the League, and partly because, as the years have passed, the Association and also the county associations have become increasingly dependent upon the financial benefits which the League clubs bring.

This difference in outlook arises because the League councillors and the county representatives are concerned with quite different things. The League representatives are there primarily to protect and, where necessary, to advance the interests of the ninety-two League clubs. These interests are likely to need reassertion with great frequency. For example, the availability of club players for international selection is a constant topic of discussion. It limits the number of internationals played; it governs the availability of an international 'squad' for training (a development with which the League is in full sympathy); and it is productive of frequent problems with the Irish, Scottish and Welsh associations, who cannot secure the release of their players who play for English clubs with the same freedom that the English association does. Possibly this inequality is felt most severely at the time when the early games in the World Cup competition are being played.

County representatives have different concerns. They have no control (other than a purely formal one which is the product of membership and support of the county FA) over Football League clubs, to whom they normally look for a handsome donation towards the ever-rising running expenses of the county association, and for the hospitality of their grounds for County Cup and Charity Cup Finals. The primary duty of a county association is to encourage, control and where necessary organise the county activities of amateur clubs at all levels. This is a task which becomes more difficult year by year. The virtual disappearance of 'gates', except for the most popular and successful amateur clubs, means that there is very little income to be derived from cup competitions, although every county runs senior and junior cup competitions for all senior and junior clubs in the county, and some of them run an 'intermediate' cup as well. A few also undertake the heavy burden of running county leagues, although this is not a task for which county association organisation is suited, and the results of such activities are not impressive. They can be supported only on the supposition that there are insufficient volunteers to undertake the task themselves, and where this situation exists the support of local senior clubs for the county league is often lukewarm. Until the final and semi-final rounds of county cup competitions, the clubs participating do so at a financial loss, although they enjoy the extra 'bite' which a knockout competition possesses, and winning the county senior cup is still a coveted honour.

Like the Football Association itself, every county association is democratic in composition. Every affiliated club is a member, and may send a representative to general meetings. Necessarily, however, policy is made by a small group whose members' length of service and frequent contacts give them a certain similarity of aims. Among the county's almost innumerable functions is the task of recruiting, classifying and controlling referees, and all referees—even Football League referees—are selected from county lists on the recommendation of county committees. The county also controls and 'sanctions' leagues whose operations are confined to one, or at most two counties. In the same way that leagues sanctioned by the Football Association are not directly represented on the FA Council, leagues sanctioned by the county associations are not directly represented in the county association's general meeting. This seems quite illogical and ought to be amended, more especially at a time when interest in football at anything below Football League level is flagging year by year.

Association football has not only the most comprehensive and complicated organisation of all outdoor sports, but it is the most regulated. It is still very much a closed world, even for an amateur player, and so far as club members who are not players are concerned, there may be a good deal of responsibility, with the possibility of a good deal of interference from above, if anything goes wrong. All clubs are under the jurisdiction of the Football Association, to whom there may be a final appeal on almost any matter; and all clubs which are not full members of the Football Association are also within the jurisdiction of the county association. This control extends, not only to all activities within the United Kingdom, but also when the club goes abroad. If a club has a dispute with another club, then Article 63 of the Articles of Association of the FA provides:

> All affiliated Associations and member Clubs, and all members of the Association, or of affiliated Associations or Clubs, shall submit and refer all differences and questions coming within the provisions of the Laws of the Game, or the Rules, Regulations and Bye-Laws of the Football Association or of the Associations to the decision of the Council who may determine the same or may appoint Committees or Commissions or other persons for the purposes of hearing and determining the same, and the fact of membership as aforesaid shall constitute an agreement to refer all such differences and questions in accordance with the Rules, Regulations and Bye-Laws of the Association, and shall be enforceable as an agreement to refer under the Arbitration Act.

All leagues and competitions must be 'sanctioned' annually, and their rules must require that all clubs, players and officials observe the rules of the FA. They may not arrange to take part in a game with any club which is not a member of the Association, or of some affiliated association, and if a person previously under the jurisdiction of the FA takes part in the activities of any unaffiliated association or club, he may not participate in football under the jurisdiction of the FA without the consent of the Council. Because of the completeness of these exclusionary provisions, which now interlock internationally, unaffiliated football has never been a serious problem for any length of time. Some years ago the sudden rise of Sunday football caused anxiety both to the FA itself and also to the county associations, more especially as it was known that a substantial number of players with regular amateur clubs were taking part in it. Sunday football has therefore been 'legalised' and is under the jurisdiction of the county associations in the usual way.

An exceedingly comprehensive group of rules defines the control which is exercised, not only over players and officials of clubs and organisations, but also over spectators. All are allowed to take part in or attend matches only on condition that they observe the rules, regulations and bye-laws of the Association, which every association and club is bound to observe and enforce. In particular, Rule 36(a) makes every association and club responsible to the Council for the actions of its players, officials and spectators, and it is required to take all precautions to prevent spectators threatening or assaulting officials before, during or at the conclusion of matches. It was for failure to discharge its duty under this rule that Leeds United and Manchester United were so severely dealt with in June 1971; but county associations (whose rules have similar provisions governing the conduct of clubs which are affiliated to the county association) are constantly dealing with incidents of lesser gravity.

The jurisdiction of the Football Association and of the county associations extends to misconduct. This is a comprehensive term, and the rules contain a number of specific items. Betting and bribery of or by players, officials, referees or linesmen are, of course, prohibited, except, in so far as betting is concerned, on registered football pools. Violating the rules of the game, or the rules and regulations of the FA, or of any affiliated organisation or league, is also misconduct, and finally, besides a number of other specified offences, the commission of 'any act not provided for above or making any statement, either verbally or in writing, or to have been responsible for conduct or any matter which, in the opinion of the Council, is likely to bring the game into disrepute.' Some day, the courts will be called upon to decide exactly how far these very general words go. They may also have to decide upon the provision in Rule 39(b), which provides: 'Any misconduct towards a referee away from the field of play will be dealt with as if the offence had been commited on the field.' Hitherto, there has been little or no appeal to the courts on matters of this kind, and there is no doubt that the wide language of Rule 40 (b) has acted as a deterrent. This rule states: 'The Rules of the Association are sufficient to enable the Council as the governing authority to deal with all cases of dispute, and legal proceedings shall only be taken as a last resort, and this only with the previous consent of the Council.'

When that rule was drafted, it was probably thought that the courts disclaimed any desire to scrutinise the proceedings of domestic tribunals. It is quite otherwise today, as will be apparent from the words of Lord Denning in the *Enderby Town FC* proceedings, which are discussed later. Meanwhile, it is apparent that no-one can be denied his right of recourse to the court if he chooses, although he will normally find it wise to proceed first through the machinery which the Football Association has provided. A further reminder that all who administer football do so within a legal framework is provided by the case of *Elliott* v. *Football Association*, reported in *The Times* of 22 October 1959. Elliott and some other professional footballers brought an action against the Football Association, claiming relief, and damages for conspiracy. In February 1959 the Football Association's solicitors sent to the footballers' solicitors an open letter offering to give the whole of the relief claimed against the Association, except the damages for the allegation of conspiracy. The Football Association then issued a summons asking that all further proceedings in the action should be halted, except such as should be necessary to give effect to the open letter, and they asked that all other proceedings should be stayed as vexatious, offensive and an abuse of the process of the court. Mr Justice Vaisey refused the claim of the Football Association, which had no right to limit the claim of the footballers by an incomplete or partial acceptance of the footballer's case.

Cases such as this one emphasise the necessity for football administrators to pay careful regard not only to the letter but also to the spirit of the rules, and to the general principles of English law. There are other branches of it, and more particularly the law of defamation, with the complexities of privilege in relation to it, which may provide traps for the unwary. It may be unfortunate but it is nevertheless true that those who today administer football would be well-advised, in case of doubt, to consult a solicitor before action is taken, especially in cases in which misconduct is alleged. For example, Rule 40(a) states:

> The Association shall be entitled to publish in the public press, or in any other manner it shall think fit, reports of its proceedings, acts and resolutions whether the same shall or shall not reflect on the character or conduct of any club, officials, player, or spectator, and every such club, official, player, or spectator, shall be deemed to have assented to such publication.

There are certain difficulties in construing the assent of a spectator, who may never have heard of the rule. In any event, the rule would not be a protection if the proceedings in respect of the allegation of misconduct had been irregularly conducted.

Proceedings arising out of charges of misconduct are governed by Rule 38(b). A member charged must receive written notice with particulars of the misconduct. To this the member must reply within seven days, asking for a personal hearing. For this the FA Council appoints a commission.

The Member charged and if necessary its Directors and

H

officials, shall attend such Hearing and give the Commission oral evidence of the facts of the charge and shall answer any questions they may ask by way of cross-examination and shall produce any books or papers they consider necessary.

The Member charged shall have the right to give and call evidence in rebuttal of the charge and shall have the right to cross-examine any witnesses who give evidence in support of such charge.

Members may not be legally represented—a matter which was also considered by Lord Denning in the Enderby Town FC case, as was also the strong flavour of criminality which pervades Rule 38. Misconduct, in a footballing sense, may also coincide with a crime—for example, with riot or breach of the peace—but if it does not, then no football legislation can add to the criminal law. The foundation of the jurisdiction exercised remains in the law of contract, to which an exceptionally wide application has been given in the organisation of football.

If one turns from the domestic to the international sphere, activity today is controlled by a number of international organisations. There has been a joint board for the four British associations since the 'nineties of last century. This has provided for the mutual recognition and protection of registrations and transfers of players, of suspensions, and of many other matters. It is this board which arranges the 'home' internationals. In addition, there is today a European Football Association, which arranges a number of inter-European club tournaments, and finally the famous FIFA (Federation International de Football Association) of which Sir Stanley Rous has been so statesmanlike a president. To the ordinary spectator, its supreme achievement must be the organisation of the World Cup Competition at four-year intervals, following the eliminating contests in the various zones into which the world has been divided. Although occasional brawls may mar the proceedings, and in doing so produce a flood of comment in the press, this tournament is an achievement comparable only with the Olympic Games for spectacle, and also for comprehensiveness of entry. It embraces the Communist and non-Communist worlds, and its existence is the final tribute to the work of the founders of the Football Association in providing a relatively simple code of laws of the game which have had an enduring appeal to most of the nations of the world. It is the more unfortunate that, after more than one attempt and the expenditure of a great deal of money, Association football has failed to establish itself firmly in either the United States of America or Canada. Perhaps it might have been better if national associations had grown naturally out of the not-inconsiderable number of amateur clubs which *do* play Association football in North America. Finally, there is Australia, which is something of a rogue elephant in the football world. A good deal of football is played there—indeed, the summer football pools upon the results of Australian games are a clear indication of this—but the clubs are mainly organised from local groups of immigrants, often of a single nationality, and no Australian national association has so far affiliated to FIFA; and no Australian team has therefore competed in the World Cup.

FIFA has also made possible the mutual recognition of national transfer systems. Article 1 of the FIFA regulations states: 'Each National Association shall determine the status and qualifications of its players, and the Federation and all affiliated Associations shall recognise such qualifications.'

The second article is also of great interest: 'Whatever may be the status of its players, a club, in order to be affiliated to one of the Associations of the Federation, shall not be used as a source of profit to its directors or shareholders. Nevertheless, in regard to the latter, the payment of a normal rate of interest is permissible.'

Compared with these national and international activities, the functions of the Football League are limited, as is also its membership. In the words of Regulation 3, 'the objects of The League are to conduct and in every respect control each season a Football Competition to be called the League Championship for each Division and at all times to safeguard the interests of the Clubs in Full and Associate Membership of The League.'

Criticisms of the management committee for not taking wide

views of football as a whole are therefore misconceived. That is not their business. It does not, however, mean that either clubs or their representatives remain in blinkers. They can and do express their views on wider questions of football interest through their representatives on the Council of the Football Association. That representation is by no means always confined to members of the management committee. Directors of League clubs are regularly elected as divisional representatives, and there are many other ways in which League clubs can and do help in the promotion of football as a whole. In the past, they have frequently organised matches with leading amateur clubs. Some enter their junior sides in lesser competitions, in which they frequently take an active interest. The picture is not necessarily an idyllic one, and it may be that there is room for some active indoctrination of some League clubs, but there is evidence that the growing problems of the amateurs are recognised by the professionals. One recent illustration of the link which may exist is the training of Skelmersdale by St John of Liverpool—a training which was of such quality that it brought Skelmersdale to two Amateur Cup Finals, on the second occasion (in 1971) successfully.

The League, like the Football Association, is a non-profit making company, and its affairs are therefore conducted in accordance with normal company practice, except that in place of a board of directors there is a committee of management. Members of this committee are elected for three years, one-third retiring annually. They are elected by ballot at the annual general meeting, and every person requires for election not less than 50 per cent of the votes of those present and entitled to vote. There may therefore be successive ballots before the necessary majority has been obtained in a particular case. In general, this procedure has ensured that there should be a good deal of continuity in the constitution of the management committee. Upsets of 'form' have been rare.

Membership of the League is divided in a way that reflects the circumstances of its growth. Full membership is confined to the clubs which have a place in either the First or the Second Division of the League. Accordingly, at the end of each season, the two full members finishing at the bottom of the Second Division surrender their status to the top two teams of the Third Division. The forty-eight members of the Third and Fourth Divisions are associate members only, and although they are fully under the jurisdiction of the League and its officers, they are represented at general meetings only in the proportion of one representative for each eleven associate members. This means that the voice of the Third and Fourth Divisions is always a subordinate one, more especially when this limitation on voting rights is considered in association with the requirement of a three-quarters' majority for the alteration of League regulations.

It is now the practice of the clubs of the Third and Fourth Divisions to meet on the eve of the League's annual general meeting, in order to reach agreement on their common interests. This ensures that their representatives in the annual general meeting are fully briefed, but it cannot affect the fact that policy is made by First and Second Division clubs.

By Regulation 15 the management committee, or any commission or sub-committee appointed by it, has power to enquire into all financial arrangements between clubs and players, and into any breach of the League's regulations, and they may impose such penalties, by way of reprimand, fine, suspension or expulsion, as they may think fit. There is also a provision for the publication of these proceedings, which is more explicit than the corresponding rule of the Football Association. It reads:

The League or the Management Committee or any duly appointed Commission or Sub-Committee shall be entitled to publish in the public press or in any other manner they shall think fit reports of their proceedings acts resolutions and findings, whether the same shall or shall not reflect on the character or conduct of any Club Official Player or spectator and all evidence tendered in such inquiries and reports shall be privileged and every such Club Official Player or spectator shall be deemed to have assented to such inquiry and to such publication and to accept the same as privileged in law.

If the statement is privileged, a person adversely affected by it will be unable to take legal action successfully in respect of it, in the absence of malice.

There is a long regulation which defines illegal inducements to players to join clubs, and which repeats the provision of the Football Association that players' contracts must be negotiated directly and not through agents—a provision which also appears in the rules of FIFA—and of all affiliated national associations and leagues.

By Regulation 19, the management committee is given power to adjudicate on all disputes other than those under Clause 18 of the contract of service (which are considered in Chapter 10); and all full and associate members agree by Regulation 21 to submit all protests, claims and complaints between them to the management committee for settlement. In both cases, there may be an appeal to a board of appeal; and for the determination of appeals under Regulation 59 (h), which arise when a club has given notice under Clause 18 (b) of the players' contract, of the terms of renewal, there is an independent tribunal of three persons:

> The chairman of the Joint Negotiating Committee for Professional Football (England and Wales) for the time being, who shall act as chairman of the tribunal.
>
> One member, or the secretary, of the Football League.
>
> One member, or the secretary, of the Professional Footballers' Association.

The relations between the Football Association and the Football League are defined in an agreement between them, which is now of long standing. This important document places in the hands of the League, but under the ultimate jurisdiction of the Association, the virtual control of professional football with the following conditions.

1. The administration and finances of the League are independent—a status not enjoyed by any other league or competition in England and Wales.

2. The president and members of the League management

committee were made members of the Council of the Association.

3. The president of the League becomes a vice-president of the Association, and also a member of the Association's Executive Committee aand International Board.

4. A joint liaison committee of the League and the Association was established to discuss matters of joint concern, and to make recommendations to the two organisations.

5. A procedure was established for dealing with breaches of rules of either organisation by League clubs. Wherever such a breach occurs, it must be reported by one organisation to the other. If it appears that the alleged breach is of the rules of the FA only, there is established an FA commission comprising an equal number of FA councillors who are members of the League management committee and councillors who are not members of the League. If a breach of League regulations only is involved, the League appoints its own commission, but there is a right of appeal to an appeals body appointed by the FA under Regulation 63.

6. All professional players must be registered with both organisations.

7. Professional players must be placed at the disposal of the FA at all times (eg, if selected for international duty).

8. International and representative matches are held in accordance with an agreed programme.

9. The League may play inter-League matches with leagues of any other national association.

10. League clubs may play matches with clubs of other national associations, but the fixtures must not clash with international or inter-League matches.

11. The programme of dates for international and inter-League matches is agreed by the FA and the League at a meeting prior to the opening of the season in which they are to be played.

12. All referees in League matches must be registered with a county association.

13. The Football League receives 4 per cent of the net gate

receipts of international and representative matches.

14. A sub-committee of the Joint Liaison Committe of the two organisations selects the matches to be televised in the ensuing season, and also negotiates for the most suitable dates, and the financial terms on which televising may occur.

What may be described as the 'auxiliary revenues' to be derived from football have achieved considerable importance in recent years—although they do not approach the importance that such rights enjoy in the United States, especially for baseball. This is primarily because the FA and the League have set their faces firmly against the televising of matches actually in progress, except at such times when it will not adversely affect the gate receipts of other matches in progress at the same time. One other major source of revenue to the Football League is derived from its copyright in the weekly fixtures which it arranges. The fact that such copyright exists was decided by Mr Justice Upjohn in *Football League Ltd* v *Littlewoods Pools Ltd*,[1] and in the course of his interesting judgement the judge set out in detail, from the evidence given by Mr Harold Sutcliffe and others, the process by which the League fixtures are compiled. No-one would deny that the operation is one of considerable skill for which the late Mr Harold Sutcliffe, like his father before him, had a special aptitude. The question to be decided was whether, once the arrangement had been made, the list which appeared was simply information, or was the subject of copyright. The judge decided that the list was copyright, of which the weekly reproduction on football pools coupons was an infringement. Since that decision, the pools promoters have paid to the Football League for the licence to use them a sum which is agreed between them.

No-one can question that the agreement between the Football Association and the League, which ended some years of friction, was a most satisfactory one from the point of view of the League, which, as the terms of the agreement show, completely protected

---

[1] [1959] 3 W.L.R. 42.

its own special interests. It is possible that it prevented a split between the professional and amateur sides of the game. The League now operates secure from intervention from those who have little knowledge of, or perhaps sympathy with, the 'big business' which top-level professional football has become. On the other hand, the interest of the League in the world of amateur football cannot be described as considerable.

From another point of view, an agreement of this kind was urgently needed, since the development of international fixtures and participation in the World Cup competition involved a completely new approach to the selection and training of the players who would be chosen. It means, above all, their association for long periods as a representative group, and for this the full co-operation of the League clubs was necessary. This has been given, and both the League and its member-clubs are now enthusiastic supporters of the policy which culminated in the appointment of Sir Alfred Ramsay as England's first full-time team manager, and in the successful campaign for the World Cup in 1966. Frequent visits abroad by club directors have done much to break down the isolation which at one period threatened to arrest the development of a modern outlook, not only upon the game itself but also upon the environment in which it was played. One further consequence of this has been that clubs have steadily developed an enthusiasm for participating in European competitions.

The League itself is a member of the International Football League Board, along with the Scottish, Northern Irish and Eire Leagues. The by-laws of this board provide for mutual recognition of players' registrations, and for transfers between clubs in different leagues. The League also arranges inter-league matches —but, unlike the Football Association, the League has not shown itself as anxious to extend inter-league games to the continent, although occasional games have been played with the Danish, Italian and Belgian Leagues. Such matches do not have the glamour of full internationals, and it is possible that the League is wise in restricting their number.

8
The Transfer System

The history of football shows that the spread of professionalism and the increasing competition for the services of professional footballers brought in its train the transfer system. Was a player free to move from club to club? Alternatively, was a professional player tied to his club until the club no longer needed him? The League's solution was to devise a system of retain-and-transfer, and although the Football Association was at first opposed to it, the essentials of what must now be called the old transfer system were settled and agreed by the beginning of the present century. By 1905, the first four-figure fee was paid, when Alf Common was transferred from Sunderland to Middlesbrough. The immediate reaction was the introduction of a rule that transfer fees should not exceed £350. This rule lasted only three months and was then rescinded, and all other suggestions to limit transfer fees have proved ineffective. Already before 1914, several fees of £2,000 and upwards had been paid. In the first years after the 1914-18 War, a proposal by the Arsenal that transfer fees should not exceed £1,650 was lost, and the Arsenal themselves were to pay the first £10,000 fee in securing David Jack from Bolton Wanderers. Since 1945, fees have continued to soar. Fees of £100,000 are now common; £160,000 has been paid, and transfers amounting to £200,000 have been discussed. The accounts of Hull City in 1971 showed that although gross gate receipts amounted to £208,905, there was a loss of £53,942 on the season. The chief reason for this was that £116,504 had been spent on the acquisition of new players in an attempt to secure promotion to the First Division—an attempt which was narrowly unsuccessful. Naturally, such spending provokes criticism, but it is not echoed with conviction by the clubs. As the accounts show, successful First Division clubs can afford this scale of expenditure—for the present at any rate. Struggling clubs hope to replenish their finances by the transfer of a talented player; and the players now can, under conditions, secure a share of the transfer fee for themselves. Nevertheless, it is quite plain that the size of modern fees is tending to concentrate the most talented players in a few wealthy and successful clubs.

Following their customary practice, both the Football Association and the Football League attempted to devise a system which, whilst being legally sound, was not likely to be challenged in the courts; and, until modern times, everyone seems to have regarded transfers as a domestic matter for the two controlling bodies. It was not until after the formation of the Professional Footballers' Union that the system was critically examined from the legal point of view. Before the Eastham case, the only occasion when the transfer system had been before the courts at all was in *Kingaby v Aston Villa Football Club*, a case very shortly reported in *The Times* of 27 March 1912. Kingaby, an Aston Villa player, wished to leave the club, which placed him on the transfer list at what he considered to be an excessive fee. He therefore sued the club for breach of contract and conspiracy. The judge refused to let the case go to the jury, as no injury or malice on the part of the club had been shown. Nobody in that case seems to have doubted the validity of the transfer system itself.

There was also a fairly recent Canadian decision which, rather strangely, was not commented on, or even mentioned, in the Eastham case. This was *Detroit Football Co v Dublinski*.[1] Dublinski was employed as a professional footballer by the plaintiffs, the football club. In his contract of service the player undertook to play for the plaintiffs, and not to play for any other club. There was also a clause giving the club an option to renew the contract at a wage not less than 90 per cent of that agreed in the original contract. At the expiration of one period of service, the player

---

[1] [1957] 7 D.L.R. (2d) 9.

signed for another club, but the employers gave notice that they intended to exercise their option to renew, without specifying the wage. It appeared that they intended to pay him the same wage as the previous season. The Ontario Court of Appeal held that the club had validly exercised its option, and that the omission of the rate of pay was not material, since it was only necessary to specify this when it was to be different from that paid previously. The absence of any discussion of this interesting case in the Eastham case is therefore to be regretted.

The transfer system as it existed before 1963 raised important questions of general law which govern the relations of employer and employee. One branch of that law has developed from the decision in *Lumley* v *Wagner*[1], a case in which a singer agreed to sing at Covent Garden for a season, and during the existence of the contract she also undertook not to sing at any other place. She quarrelled with the management and left whilst the contract was in existence, and the court granted the manager of Covent Garden an injunction preventing her from appearing anywhere else during the season covered by the contract. The whole of this branch of the law was discussed in *Warner Bros* v *Nelson*.[2] In that case, Warner Bros were seeking to enforce a clause in their contract of service with Miss Nelson (otherwise the famous film actress, Bette Davies) which prohibited her, so long as the contract existed, from acting for any other film company. There was also another clause giving the company the right to extend the period of its operation for one equivalent to that during which the actress refused or neglected to act for them. It was argued that the clause was in undue restraint of trade and void. On this the judge (Branson, J) said:

> The ground for this contention was that the contract compelled the defendant to serve the plaintiffs exclusively, and might in certain circumstances endure for the whole of her natural life. No authority was cited to me in support of the proposition that such a contract is illegal, and I see no reason for so holding. Where, as in the present contract, the covenants are all concerned with what is to happen whilst the defendant is

---

[1] [1852] 21 L.J.Ch. 898.   [2] [1937] I K.B. 209.

employed by the plaintiffs and not thereafter, there is no room
for the application of the doctrine of restraint of trade.

So far as employers and employees are concerned, therefore,
the doctrine of restraint of trade is only relevant in relation to
clauses in a contract which are designed to protect the employer
from competition by the employee for a limited period or in a
limited area afterwards, or which protects him from the dis-
closure of trade secrets, or possibly from special skills which the
employee has gained in the employer's service. All such re-
straints must be reasonable, which means substantially that they
must not be wider in scope than is necessary to protect the
employer's business.

It is against this background that the transfer system which
formerly existed should be tested. By the rules of the Football
Association (Rule 25) every professional player must be registered with the Association before he could play for his club.
Contracts were made for twelve months, and every player must
be re-registered before the beginning of a new season before he
was eligible to play.

By Rule 26 (b) a club wishing to retain a player must give him
notice of its intention to retain him between May and the first
Saturday in June. It must also inform the player that he would
be paid at the rate of £418 a year. Notice of the intention to
retain must also be given to the Football Association, which had
power to refuse it if the club's offer did not provide a reasonable
remuneration for the player. A retained player remained the
registered player of the retaining club until he satisfied the council of the Football Association that there were special grounds
why he should be allowed to change his club. So long as he was
retained, he was not free to play for another club. If he did, this
would amount to misconduct, for which either the club or the
Association might impose penalties.

A professional player could be transferred from one club to
another by agreement of both clubs, and with the player's own
consent. He was only free to seek employment with another club
when his contract had ended and he had not been retained. It

should be added that the ban on employment would extend not only to clubs affiliated to the English, Scottish, Welsh, Irish and Northern Irish Associations, but also to all clubs affiliated to associations which are members of FIFA. As Mr Justice Wilberforce described it in the Eastham case, 'once a professional player has been registered with a Football Association club he could, if and so long as the club with which he was registered desired to retain him, be prevented from being transferred to any other club and be prevented from seeking any employment as a professional footballer anywhere in the world'—except in one of the very few countries where the clubs were not affiliated to FIFA.

The rules of the Football League were supplementary to those of the Football Association. Players were also registered with the League, and both for registration and transfer there were (and are) appropriate forms. By the closing day of each season League clubs must forward to the League two lists: the first, the retained list, containing the names of the players they wished to retain, and the transfer list, which contained the names of those whom they were prepared to transfer, and also the amount of the transfer fee expected. The retentions and the transfer systems might operate separately or together, the transfer list enabling the transfer fees to be obtained and the retained list enabling the club, provided that it offered a reasonable wage, to hold on to the player until either he re-signed with that club or it received an offer for him which it considered acceptable. A player could be retained without being put on the transfer list, or be put on the transfer list without being retained, or he could be put on both; at the end of his year of service, if not again registered, retained or put on the transfer list, he was free.

If a player was dissatisfied with the terms offered for his retention or with the transfer fee which the club was asking for him, or if the club was unable to get his club to agree to transfer him, he had a right to appeal to the management committee. Regulation 62(e) of the League's regulations gave the League power to adjudicate in these cases, and Regulation 19 obliged the League to adjudicate on any difference or dispute between a club and a player on the application of either party. It was pointed out in the Eastham case that, between 1956 and 1963, there had been 499 appeals, from which 259 players had obtained a free transfer and 123 had succeeded in getting their transfer fees reduced.

There was no doubt that players resented this system as a one-sided arrangement which placed the clubs in a dominating position. On the other hand, the clubs had always insisted on its maintenance, as without it, or something like it, there would be a continuing tendency for players to move from club to club, and particularly to the larger and wealthier clubs. There was a further point of some importance. The players had consistently contended for longer contracts than annual ones, but the clubs had continued to insist upon annual engagements with an indefinite option for renewal.

It is against this background that the extremely important case of *Eastham* v *Newcastle United Football Club*[1] must be considered. The plaintiff, George Eastham, originally played for Ards, in Northern Ireland, first as an amateur, and then, on reaching the age of nineteen, as a professional. In 1956 he was transferred from Ards to Newcastle United for a fee £9,000. Thereafter, he re-signed annually, the last occasion being on 1 July 1959. This renewal would have expired on 30 June 1960. However, in consequence of differences which had arisen between the player and the club, he asked on 11 December 1960 to be put on the transfer list. No formal answer was given to him, but the chairman of the club assured him that he was looking for a job for the player, and that work was being done to a house which he would be able to rent. On 29 April 1960 (which was two days before the first date specified in the League rule) the club notified him that he would be retained for the following season at the same wage, and the League was informed of this. The player did not re-sign, and on 23 June the club informed him that he had been retained

---

[1] [1963] 3 W.L.R. 574

under Rule 26(b) of the Football Association's rules. Two days later the player renewed his application to be put on the transfer list, and this was rejected by the Newcastle board on 29 June. On 4 July the player left Newcastle and went to work for a company in Surrey, and ten days later he applied to the League's management committee under Rule 26(e), stating that he was unable to arrange his transfer with the club and asking for the League's permission to transfer. A week later the club wrote to the League, pointing out that they had kept strictly to the rules and expressing the hope that the management committee would uphold their action. On 23 July the management committee considered the player's appeal and decided that the matter was entirely between the club and the player. There were further letters and interviews, but the dispute dragged on until October, during which statements in the press gave the player the impression that the club would continue to retain him. Since Eastham had not re-signed by the beginning of the season, he was no longer being paid. Finally, on 13 October a writ was issued on behalf of the player alleging that the club had deprived and was still depriving him of the opportunity to earn his living by playing professional football, that in doing so the club were acting in unlawful restraint of trade, and claiming damages. Actually, by the time the action was tried, the club had at long last consented to transfer Eastham to the Arsenal.

The judgment delivered by Mr Justice Wilberforce decided that the retention provisions, which operated after a player's employment had ended, and not as an option causing the employment to continue, substantially interfered with the player's right to seek employment. It therefore was in restraint of trade and unenforceable. So far as the transfer system, as then operating, was concerned, this was not equally objectionable, but when it was allied to this system of retention, the two together operated in restraint of trade, since they went beyond what was reasonable to protect the interests of the club.

During the hearing, a good deal of evidence had been heard —from the club, from the Football Association, the Football

League, and finally from Cliff Lloyd, the secretary of the Players' Union. Some of it is considered in the course of the judgment in which, in effect, the whole working of professional football was reviewed.

> The transfer system [said the judge] has been stigmatised by the plaintiff's counsel as a relic from the Middle Ages, involving the buying and selling of human beings as chattels; and, indeed, to anyone not hardened to acceptance of the practice it would seem inhuman, and incongruous to the spirit of a national sport. One must not forget that the consent of a player to the transfer is necessary, but, on the other hand, the player has little security since he cannot get a long-term contract and, while he is on the transfer list awaiting an offer, his feelings and anxieties as to who his next employer is to be may not be very pleasant. The defendants and their directors—such of them, at least, who appeared before me—reasonable men whose attitude to the players was as much paternal as proprietary, have evolved a euphemistic description of the transfer fee which apparently satisfies their consciences. They do not 'sell' players, they receive compensation for the transfer of the registration. In this case I am not called on to choose between descriptions of the practice; all I have to decide is whether the plaintiff's attack on the system as opposed to a recognised principle of English law can succeed.

Somewhat earlier the judge had described the transfer system as unique in the field of sport, but later he commented on its broader aspects. Many of the national associations within FIFA have a transfer system; retention was the decisive element in the Canadian decision to which reference has already been made; and, finally, American baseball contains it. This failed to impress the judge, however. He commented:

> The system is an employers' system, set up in an industry where the employers have succeeded in establishing a united monolithic front all over the world, and where it is clear that for the purpose of negotiation the employers all over the world consider the system a good system, but this does not prevent the court from considering whether it goes further than is reasonably necessary to protect their legitimate interests.

The relation between the Football Association and the League was most felicitously summarised in the following passage:

I

[The position of the Football Association] is one of support of the League's case, but a somewhat reserved support. The Association, originally formed in the 1860s to secure a uniform code of rules, came up against professionalism in football towards the end of the century. Its first concern was to establish a distinction between amateurs and professionals, and this was the origin of the requirement of registration. Then there came the abuse of poaching. The Association dealt with this by restricting players to one club, and by a rule permitting retention. Beyond this the Football Association has always been reluctant to go. It has always dissociated itself from the finances of professional football and taken a neutral position as between employers and employees. In the proceedings which took place in 1952 under the Conciliation Act, 1896, which resulted in the Foster Report, the Association's position was that it had no objection to contracts for longer than a year, and was not concerned with any maximum wage; that generally on financial matters and on restriction on the movement of players, the Association aligned itself with the League, but could not stand aside if they thought there was any reason for discontent. . . .

So that this view of the Association—and I think it is not without importance, since the Association takes rather a broader view than the League and its members—is really this, that having left to the League responsibility in financial matters, it [the Association] is not prepared to differ from the opinion formed by the League, in a matter within their competence, that the transfer fee system is a vital necessity. It does not, by its own evidence and of its own independent opinion, support the system.

Some of the evidence commented on in the judgment is worthy of examination in the light of after events. Mr Lloyd, on behalf of the Players' Union, had contended that the removal of the maximum wage had been very beneficial, and that players were less tempted to look for outside jobs, and were more inclined to give all their energies to the game. It is true that the life of the professional footballer has become more strenuous, as competition has become fiercer, but at no previous time have leading players been more involved in outside activities than they are today. It was urged by Mr Hardaker, for the Football League, that if the retention system were abandoned, there would be a concentration of professional football in a few large centres. The judge completely rejected this prediction, which has not happened—yet. Nevertheless, the evidence which appears earlier in this book shows that the gap between the wealthy club in the large city and the smaller ones in lower divisions of the League has widened since the maximum wage was abolished; and the indications are that this will continue.

The judge accepted the proposition that the retention system had in the past prevented poaching; but he thought that the answer to this lay in longer contracts—a solution which clubs are naturally reluctant to adopt.

On behalf of the League, it had been suggested that the system maintained a uniform standard of play between the clubs in various divisions, in that the good players were spread more or less evenly. This suggestion has more relevance to a maximum wage than to the retain-and-transfer system, and the judge did not accept it. Nevertheless, present tendencies are quite plain.

The decision in this case for practical purposes ended the old retain-and-transfer system which, it may be suggested, had become out of harmony with changing conceptions of the proper relationship between employer and employee. On the whole, the effects of the decision have been less disruptive than the Football League feared they might be, and it is also apparent that the position of a modern player of the highest ability does not compare unfavourably with that of his counterpart abroad, except perhaps in Brazil, where the great Pele receives rather more respect, and a vastly higher salary, than the President. The transfer system remains one of the cornerstones of the professional game, and the club still exercises an option to renew the agreement for one or more years. A club may exercise such an option in respect of a player whose registration they wish to transfer, and the club must still send to the League a list of players, together with a statement of those whom it is prepared to transfer. Where a club informs the player of its intention to re-engage him, the player must give notice of his acceptance within twenty-eight days. If he has not re-signed by 30 June, a dispute is automatically deemed to exist between the player and his club and either party may ask the League management committee to adjudicate on it before 31 July. From this decision there may be a further appeal to an independent tribunal, which itself must decide before 30 September. League Regulation 59 (d) provides, however, that until a new contract is signed or until the final determination of the appeal, the existing contract of service is prolonged between the club and the player.

There has been a further major change in the operation of the transfer system. Where a player is transferred at the request of his club, the transfer fee is subject to a deduction of 10 per cent with a minimum of £500. One half of this is paid to the Football League Provident Fund, the other half is paid to the player himself. If, on the other hand, the player is transferred at his own request, he only receives his share of the 10 per cent if the management committee of the League are satisfied that his request for transfer was made on reasonable grounds.

Finally, there was a sequel to the Eastham case in the decision of Mr Justice Foster in *Cooke* v *Football Association* in March 1972. By the rules of the international association of Football Associations (FIFA) a professional player under contract cannot leave his national association for a club under the jurisdiction of another association, whilst under contract to his club and whilst he is under the jurisdiction of that club's association. Although the rules of the English Football Association and Football League were changed in consequence of the Eastham case, this did not affect foreign associations, whose rules have for the most part remained unaltered. In particular, the rules of the Eire Football Association remain unchanged. John Cooke, a professional player of Sligo Rovers, a club under the jurisdiction of the Eire FA, was retained by them with a £1,000 transfer fee, but wanted to join Wigan Borough, an English non-League club. In pursuance of the rules of FIFA, the English FA refused registration of this player for seventeen weeks during the 1970-71 season, pending clearance by the Irish Association, and he therefore sued the English FA. Mr Justice Foster decided that the FIFA rule amounted to a restraint of trade, invalid by English law, and was therefore inoperative. He said:

It was said that if in this case the FA had given Cooke permission to play and registered him without a transfer certificate it would have been suspended from FIFA or disaffiliated. I agree that the consequences to English football, both amateur and professional, would have been grave if that had occurred, since no English club, amateur or professional, could play abroad.

He added that he did not think that the result of the case would be the expulsion of the English FA from FIFA, yet the risk remains until the FIFA rule is modified, and modification will involve the consent of all member associations, now numbering approximately a hundred.

9
Disciplinary Procedures and Natural Justice

The complex code of football rules is enforced by the possibility of disciplinary proceedings at all stages. Sometimes there is a special committee which is charged with the duty of determining these questions. Sometimes it is the management committee of the organisation which disposes of them. Further, there may exist the possibility of an appeal to some other body. The rules of the league in which a club plays will invariably contain one or more rules which deal with the obligations of players and clubs, and the procedure by which these obligations are enforced. Sometimes, too, the rules include an express statement that, in joining, a club contracts with the league to fulfil its obligations, and to submit its disputes with other clubs to the management committee for determination. Whether this is so stated or not, the position is the same. In law, the league exercises its powers to decide in virtue of the contract between the league, the club and the club's members. The latter are bound by the action of the club, whether incorporated as a company or not, in joining. So far as a club which is incorporated is concerned, the action of the directors in securing admission to a league is governed by the ordinary rules of company law, which give powers to directors to act on behalf of the company. Where, as is the case with most amateur clubs, there is no incorporation, the authority of the secretary and committee is derived from their election by members of the club, to whom also many important questions affecting the club may be directly referred by the committee.

By the rules of the Football Association, the rules of the league must contain a provision for member clubs and their players to appeal from a decision of the league to some other body. If the league functions within the area of a county, or of two counties only, and has been sanctioned by the county association, the appeals will be heard by an appeals committee set up by the county football association of the club which is appealing. Where there is an appeal from the decision of a league operating over a wider area, and which therefore is sanctioned by the Football Association itself, there will be an appeal to the Football Association direct.

This, however, is by no means all. Every club must be affiliated to a county football association and, by affiliating, it undertakes to accept the rules of the association. These, in turn, establish a code of conduct for the clubs within the county's jurisdiction. Moreover, it is the county which hears and determines all complaints of misconduct by players upon the field of play within their area. In addition, the county is responsible for ensuring that a club observes all the rules applicable to it—for example, rules relating to its constitution, the keeping of proper accounts, the holding of annual meetings, and many other matters. Sometimes a major dispute with the county may blow up from a difference which was originally quite trifling. These are decided by the county, unless the club is in direct membership with the Football Association, when the dispute will go directly to the Football Association. Even in those cases in which the county association has jurisdiction, there is a right of appeal to the Football Association.

All this sounds highly complicated, and it certainly proves to be so in practice. It may become even more complicated if there are also disputes about the competence of the body—whether league or county association—which is exercising jurisdiction. Today, clubs and players are alert in the defence of their rights and are not inclined to let anything go by default. It has been pointed out that the traditional attitude of the Football Association has been paternalistic. It has existed upon the foundation that their decisions are in the best interests of the game. This also is questioned today, with the result that what it does is scrutinised more closely than ever before.

One result of this has been a plain tendency for both clubs and players to test their rights in court. It has taken them a long time to get there, and to realise that football does not exist in a vacuum. As with every other social activity, it exists only within the limits permitted by the law. Now that this major fact has been appreciated, there will be a succession of decisions, and it may be that rules which have existed almost from the first days of association will have to be modified, as the transfer system already has been. Startling as it may appear to football legislators and administrators, their actions may be challenged in court at any time, and today, when so much money is invested in football, in vital matters players and clubs will not be content until they have exhausted all the remedies which are open to them.

In this respect they are following in the steps of members of some other large voluntary associations—for example, trade unions, or other associations of sportsmen or societies and clubs —and a large body of case-law defining the rights of members and the conduct of disciplinary committees has been progressively developed. Traditionally, the attitude of English law has been in favour of allowing the largest possible autonomy to such voluntary associations, but there are some over-riding principles which are based on public policy. One of them is that the rights enjoyed by members are preserved. Another is that in proceedings affecting those rights, the principles of fair play—or to give it its more usual description in the modern cases, of natural justice—are observed. This is now particularly apparent where the body which is sitting in judgement can make a decision which affects the livelihood of the person whose conduct is under scrutiny. In such proceedings the jurisdiction of the courts cannot be ousted, notwithstanding any provision in the rules to the contrary. Any such provision, as will be evident in the discussion of two recent cases which appears below, is null and void as contrary to public policy. From this point of view football leagues and associations are in a position which in no way differs from that of any other voluntary association. It is important, therefore, that they should not only scrutinise their rules carefully with these considerations in mind, but that they should also examine procedures in their disciplinary and allied proceedings to ensure that they satisfy the tests which the law imposes. These, though not technical, are fundamental.

The clearest and most authoritative exposition of the relation of the courts to the domestic tribunals of associations of all kinds is to be found in the well-known judgement of Lord Justice Denning (as he then was) in the Court of Appeal in *Lee* v *The Showmen's Guild of Great Britain*.[1] Lee was a member of the Guild, which was a trade union of travelling showmen, and he had been involved in a dispute with the Guild over his right to use a particular site which had been allotted to him by the local corporation, but which the area committee of the Guild had allotted to another, and rival showman. After hearing the dispute the committee of the Guild decided that he had broken one of the rules, and fined him. Lee refused to pay the fine, whereupon the Guild invoked another rule and expelled him. Lee thereupon challenged the committee's actions in the courts, and the Court of Appeal decided that the action of the committee, together with the fines and expulsion which they had imposed, were *ultra vires* (ie, beyond its lawful authority) and void.

Much of Lord Justice Denning's judgement is concerned with the principles applicable to situations such as this, and it must be understood by all who participate in proceedings of this kind. He says:

> The jurisdiction of a domestic tribunal, such as the committee of the Showmen's Guild, must be founded on a contract, express or implied. Outside the regular courts of this country, no set of men can sit in judgment on their fellows except so far as Parliament authorizes it or the parties agree to it. The jurisdiction of the committee of the Showmen's Guild is contained in a written set of rules to which all the members subscribe. This set of rules contains the contract between the members and is just as much subject to the jurisdiction of these courts as any other contract.

---

[1] [1952] 2 Q.B. 329.

It was once said ... that the courts only intervened in these cases to protect rights of property ... but Fletcher Moulton L.J. denied that there was any such limitation to the power of the courts ... and it has now become clear that he was right. .... The power of this court to intervene is founded on the jurisdiction to protect rights of contract. If a member is expelled by a committee in breach of contract, this court will grant a declaration that their action is *ultra vires*. It will also grant an injunction to prevent his expulsion if that is necessary to protect a proprietary right of his; or to protect him in his right to earn his livelihood; but it will not grant an injunction to give a member the right to enter a social club, unless there are proprietary rights attached to it, because it is too personal to be specifically enforced. .... That is, I think, the only relevance of rights of property in this connexion. It goes to the form of remedy, not to the right.

Although the jurisdiction of a domestic tribunal is founded on contract, express or implied, nevertheless the parties are not free to make any contract they like. There are important limitations imposed by public policy. The tribunal must, for instance, observe the principles of natural justice. They must give the man notice of the charge and a reasonable opportunity of meeting it. Any stipulation to the contrary would be invalid. They cannot stipulate for a power to condemn a man unheard. .... Another limitation arises out of the well-known principle that the parties cannot by contract oust the ordinary courts from their jurisdiction. .... They can, of course, agree to leave questions of law, as well as questions of fact, to the decision of the domestic tribunal. They can, indeed, make the tribunal the final arbiter on question of fact, but they cannot make it the final arbiter on questions of law. They cannot prevent its decisions being examined by the courts. If parties should seek, by agreement, to take the law out of the hands of the courts and put it into the hands of a private tribunal, without any recourse at all to the courts in case of error of law, then the agreement is to that extent contrary to public policy and void. ...

The question in this case is: to what extent will the courts examine the decisions of domestic tribunals on points of law? This is a new question which is not to be solved by turning to the club cases. In the case of social clubs, the rules usually empower the committee to expel a member who, in their opinion, has been guilty of conduct detrimental to the club; and this is a matter of opinion and nothing else. The courts have no wish to

sit on appeal from their decisions on such a matter any more
than from decisions of a family conference. They have nothing to
do with social rights or social duties. On any expulsion they will
see that there is fair play. They will see that the man has notice
of the charge and a reasonable opportunity of being heard. They
will see that the committee observe the procedures laid down by
the rules; but they will not otherwise interfere. . . .

It is very different with domestic tribunals which sit in
judgment on the members of a trade or profession. They wield
powers as great as, if not greater than, any exercised by the
courts of law. They can deprive a man of his livelihood. They
can ban him from the trade in which he has spent his life and
which is the only trade he knows. They are usually empowered
to do this for any breach of their rules, which, be it noted,
are rules which they impose and which he has no real opportunity of accepting or rejecting. In theory their powers are based
on contract. The man is supposed to have contracted to give
them these great powers; but in practice he has no choice in the
matter. If he is to engage in the trade, he has to submit to the
rules promulgated by the committee. Is such a tribunal to be
treated by these courts on the same footing as a social club? I
say no. A man's right to work is just as important to him as, if
not more important than, his rights of property. These courts
intervene every day to protect rights of property. They must also
intervene to protect his right to work.

But the question still remains: to what extent will the courts
intervene? They will, I think, always be prepared to examine the
decision to see that the tribunal has observed the law. This includes the correct interpretation of the rules. Let me give an
illustration. If a domestic tribunal is given power by the rules to
expel a member for misconduct, such as here for 'unfair competition', does that mean that the tribunal is the sole judge of what
constitutes unfair competition? Suppose it puts an entirely
wrong construction on the words 'unfair competition' and finds
a member guilty of it when no reasonable person could so find,
has not the man a remedy? I think he has, for the simple reason
that he has only agreed to the committee exercising jurisdiction
according to the true interpretation of the rules, and not
according to a wrong interpretation. . . . The courts have never
allowed a master to dismiss a servant except in accordance with
the terms of the contract between them. So also they cannot
permit a domestic tribunal to deprive a member of his livelihood

or to injure him in it, unless the contract, on its true construction, gives the tribunal power to do so.

I repeat 'on its true construction' because I desire to emphasise that the true construction of the contract is to be decided by the courts and by no-one else. . . . The rules are the contract between the members. The committee cannot extend their jurisdiction by giving a wrong interpretation to the contract, no matter how honest they may be. They have only such jurisdiction as the contract on its true interpretation confers on them, not what they think it confers. The scope of their jurisdiction is a matter for the courts, and not for the parties, let alone for one of them. . . .

In most of the cases which come before such a domestic tribunal, the task of the committee can be divided into two parts: firstly, they must construe the rules; secondly, they must apply the rules to the facts. The first is a question of law which they must answer correctly if they are to keep within their jurisdiction; the second is a question of fact which is essentially a matter for them. The whole point of giving jurisdiction to a committee is so that they can determine the facts and decide what is to be done about them. The two parts of the task are, however, often inextricably mixed together. The construction of the rules is so bound-up with the application of the rules to the facts that no-one can tell one from the other. When that happens, the question whether the committee has acted within its jurisdiction depends, in my opinion, on whether the facts adduced before them were reasonably capable of being held to be a breach of rules. If they were, then the proper inference is that the committee correctly construed the rules and have acted within their jurisdiction. If, however, the facts were not reasonably capable of being held to be a breach, and yet the committee held them to be a breach, then the only inference is that the committee have misconstrued the rules and exceeded their jurisdiction. The proposition is sometimes stated in the form that the court can interfere if there was evidence to support the finding of the committee; but that only means that the facts were not reasonably capable of supporting the finding.

In the two decades which have elapsed since Lord Denning gave this very notable judgement, its principles have been regularly applied in other actions arising from the activities of domestic tribunals, which may be regarded as being regularly under the watchful scrutiny of the courts in an ever widening range. For example, the action of the vice-chancellor, in fining and excluding a student for a year from a university for misconduct, was held to be of such a judicial character that the requirements of natural justice set out by Lord Denning must necessarily be satisfied.[1] They were invoked recently by the Court of Appeal in another trade union case of special importance, *Breen* v *Amalgamated Engineering Union*,[2] in which Lord Denning (now Master of the Rolls) again delivered a vigorous judgement, taking his earlier decision in Lee's case a stage further. Breen had been elected a shop steward by his fellow members, but the district committee of his union refused to approve his election, so that under the rules he was unable to act. No reasons were given for this refusal. Breen protested and asked for the matter to be reconsidered, whereupon the committee reaffirmed its decision, and in furnishing him with reasons made allegations about him which he had had no opportunity of answering. All the members of the Court of Appeal were of opinion that the committee was under a duty to act fairly, but if it acted in good faith, the court would not disturb its decision. Lord Denning thought that the committee's decision, being based on invalid reasons, ought to be declared itself invalid. In comparing the position of domestic committees with those of statutory bodies, he said:

> The judge[3] held that it was not open to the courts to review the decision of the district committee: because they were not exercising a judicial or quasi-judicial function. It was entirely a matter for discretion whether Mr Breen was approved or not. It could be vitiated if it was made in bad faith, but not otherwise. And he declined to find bad faith.
>
> In so holding, the judge was echoing views which were current some years ago. But there have been important developments in the last twenty-two years which have transformed the situation.

Lord Denning then described what was required by law in the case of a statutory body entrusted by statute with a discretion,

---

[1] *Glynn* v *Keele University* [1971] 1 W.L.R. 487.   [2] [1971] 2 W.L.R. 742.
[3] Cusack, J., who had first tried the case.

particularly emphasising the importance of the decision of the House of Lords in *Padfield* v *Minister of Agriculture, Fisheries and Food*[1] on this point. He continued:

> Does all this apply also to a domestic body? I think it does, at any rate when it is a body set up by one of the powerful associations which we see nowadays. Instances are readily to be found in the books, notably the Stock Exchange, the Jockey Club, the Football Association, and innumerable trade unions. All these delegate power to committees. These committees are domestic bodies which control the destinies of thousands. They have quite as much power as the statutory bodies of which I have been speaking. They can make or mar a man by their decisions, not only by expelling him from membership, but also by refusing to admit him as a member; or, it may be, by refusal to grant a licence or to give their approval. Often their rules are framed so as to give them a discretion. They then claim that it is an 'unfettered' discretion with which the courts have no right to interfere. They go too far. They claim too much. The Minister made the same claim in the Padfield case, and was roundly rebuked by the House of Lords for his impudence. So should we treat their claim by trade unions. They are not above the law, but subject to it. Their rules are said to be a contract between the members and the union. So be it. If they are a contract, then it is an implied term that the discretion should be exercised fairly. But the rules are in reality more than a contract. They are a legislative code laid down by the council of the union to be obeyed by the members. This code should be subject to control by the courts just as much as a code laid down by Parliament itself. If the rules set up a domestic body and give it a discretion, it is to be implied that the body must exercise its discretion fairly. Even though its functions are not judicial or quasi-judicial, but only administrative, still it must act fairly. Should it not do so, the courts can review its decision, just as it can review the decision of a statutory body. The courts cannot grant prerogative writs such as *certiorari* and *mandamus* against domestic bodies, but they can grant declarations and injunctions, which are the modern machinery for enforcing administrative law.

Several comments may be made on this decision. The first is that although the other two members of the Court of Appeal did

---

[1] [1968] A.C. 997.

not go as far as Lord Denning in holding that the trade union committee's decision in this instance should be invalidated and the union made liable, both were of opinion that the committee must act fairly, and both expressed regret that they could not help a litigant who 'on any view, has been grossly abused'. They, nevertheless, felt that they were prevented from helping him simply because, in the circumstances, they felt unable to disturb the trial judge's findings of fact. Although this was sufficient to defeat the plaintiff's claim in this case, it is obviously not the end of this question. Lord Denning has frequently been a dissenting minority in one case, only to be proved right in a later one, and his contention that domestic bodies should be subject to the same limitations in the exercise of their discretions as statutory bodies has considerable force, and may well prove to be the true principle in the long run. In the meanwhile, domestic bodies exercising discretions would be well advised to act with due regard to the requirements of natural justice.

It will have been noticed that Lord Denning included the Football Association among those bodies whose rules confer on its committees wide powers to affect the livelihood of many persons. In recent years, these have for the first time been tested in the courts, as the powers of the Scottish Football Association also have been.

In *Keighley Rugby Football Club* v *Cunningham*, a case briefly reported in *The Times* of 25 May 1960, the disciplinary committee and the appeals committee of the Rugby Football League had suspended a player, following an episode in a cup-tie on 13 February 1960, following which the player was sent off. Danckwerts J. decided that the suspension was invalid, on the ground that it was contrary to natural justice, because the committee had suspended the player without giving him a hearing or any other opportunity to clear his name.

In *St Johnstone Football Club Ltd* v *Scottish Football Association Ltd*,[1] the club sought a declaration that a censure and fine

---

[1] (1965) *Scots Law Times* 171.

imposed on them by the Executive and General Purposes Committee of the Scottish FA was *ultra vires* and void.

In October 1963, St Johnstone decided to arrange a benefit match for one of their players, named Carr. The permission of the Scottish Football Association was needed, the club therefore made the usual application and the match was played, but it was the occasion of lengthy correspondence between the club and the association, relating principally to the manner in which the arrangements for the match had been made. Some time after the match the club received a letter from the Scottish FA which said:

> The Executive and General Purposes Committee have now had an opportunity of considering the correspondence which has passed between us in this connection. They are surprised that, notwithstanding the warning which you were given in January 1962, you should again place in the hands of the St Johnstone Aid Club a considerable part of the arrangements. It has been decided that your club be severely censured and fined £25. Please let me have your remittance.

Further correspondence followed, and on 6 April 1964, the Association wrote to the club as follows:

> I have to inform you that your letter of the 19th ultimo was placed before the Executive and General Purposes Committee on Wednesday last, and I am instructed to tell you that their decision was confirmed by Council at their last meeting, at which, if your club were dissatisfied, they should have arranged to have it challenged.

The club, in reply stated that they had received no notice of the meeting of the Council, and that in any event there was no provision in the Scottish FA's articles of association to review the decision, and again asked for the Council's decision to be reconsidered. This was refused, and the Council asked that the fine of £25 should be paid without further delay. The club therefore instituted an action to have the decision to censure and to fine declared *ultra vires* and void, and asked for the production of the minutes of the meeting in which the Council's decision had been reached, arguing that in reaching it, the Council and the General Purposes Committee had acted contrary to the principles of natural justice. In respect of both proceedings they contended:

1. That they did not know, and were not informed, that any charge was being considered against them by the committee.

2. They were not told what was the nature of the charge that was being made against them.

3. They were not given any opportunity of meeting the charge, nor were they informed of the date of the meeting, so that they could lay evidence before the committee.

4. Finally, they were not given any opportunity to attend the meetings, or make any representations to them.

The club added that they were not given notice of the rule they were alleged to have broken until four days before the meeting of the Council, so that the notice was insufficient for them to prepare a statement. In addition, they stated that there was no provision in the articles of association of the Scottish FA for decisions of the committee to be appealed to the Council.

At the hearing before Lord Kilbrandon, the Association admitted that the allegations made by the club were true, and it therefore followed that the proceedings conflicted with the principles of natural justice. The argument therefore turned upon the question whether the club had a right of action at all, and the Association contended that it had no such right since the club, in terms of Scottish law, had suffered no patrimonial loss, which (it was argued) was necessary before a court of law could review proceedings arising from decisions of committees of voluntary associations. A patrimonial loss may, for this purpose, be regarded as a legally enforceable right against the club, and a line of Scottish cases in which this question was considered was examined by the judge. The judge, however, drew attention to Rule 135 of the Association, which gave it the 'right to fine, suspend or expel a club in default', and pointed out that the effect of this was to make a penalty, if properly imposed, a civil debt, recoverable at law. This, therefore, amounted to a patri-

K

monial loss, giving the club the right to institute proceedings to have the decision set aside, if improperly reached.

This highly interesting judgement also dealt with two other matters. The judge pointed out that the Association had admitted that its action was inconsistent with the principles of natural justice.

> That is [he said], as I think, something which goes far beyond a mere allegation of *ultra vires* or of unwarrantable departure from authorised procedure. I entertain no doubt that one of the inferences to be drawn from Article 135 is that the Council, when exercising the powers which it was agreed to confer upon them, must do so in a judicial spirit, for the very good reason that the article in question purports to constitute them into some kind of a judicial body. They are actually described in the article as 'judges' and one of the powers which they can exercise is that of imposing 'fines'.

Secondly, the judge drew attention to Article 75, which purported to prevent clubs from taking legal proceedings on any matter without the previous consent of the Council. This, said the judge, can only have a very limited application, ie, to matters which can only be decided by the Council, eg, matters of procedure. It could not in any way abridge the right of recourse to the courts in any matter involving legal rights. If the rule were intended to mean anything else, it would be void, as contrary to public policy. Accordingly, the action of the St Johnstone Club was well-founded, and succeeded.

The question of access to the courts was again one of the matters raised in a later English case, *Enderby Town Football Club Ltd v Football Association Ltd*.[1] This was an appeal by the club against a decision of Foster J., and once again Lord Denning, Master of the Rolls, delivered the leading judgement, with which the other two members of the court agreed.

The case arose out of an investigation undertaken by the Leicester and Rutland FA, which is of course affiliated to the Football Association, into the affairs of the Enderby Town Foot-

---

[1] [1970] 3 W.L.R. 1021.

ball Club, which is a limited company with its own memorandum and articles of association. The club is run (in the words of Lord Denning) 'on commercial lines'. Directors were paid £700 a year each and their expenses. In addition, it runs a totalisator, on which the members of the public can bet. All followers of football will know that these activities are out of line with present football practice, and accordingly, the Leicester FA appointed a three-man commission to hear charges of irregularities against the club. At a hearing on 5 May 1970, attended by three directors of the club and its secretary, the commission found that there had been gross negligence in its administration. They therefore fined the club £500, severely censured it and the directors, and ordered them to take immediate steps to reorganise the club in accordance with the rules of the FA.

The club appealed to the FA, and its solicitor asked for permission to be represented by solicitor and counsel at the hearing of the appeal. This was refused, and on 8 July 1970 the club issued a writ, asking for an injunction to restrain the FA from hearing the appeal unless the club was permitted to be legally represented. This was refused by Mr Justice Foster.

Rule 38(b) of the FA's rules states:

> An association, competition or club may be represented at the hearing of an appeal, complaint or claim, or at an enquiry, by one or more of its members. A barrister or solicitor may only represent an association, competition or club of which he is a member, if he be chairman or secretary. Any person summoned to attend an enquiry or the hearing of an appeal, complaint or claim must attend personally and not be legally represented.

For the club, it was argued that if the rule in fact excluded legal representation, it ought not be applied in this case, because there were complex legal points to be decided. Of these, the main ones were:

1. The charge against the club was not properly formulated. The first count was 'that directors' fees were paid' to the directors, without pointing to any rule which says that fees may not be paid. In fact there was no such rule. Rule 45(vi) of the FA,

it was argued, extends only to clubs in membership with the (national) FA. Enderby Town was not so affiliated. It was a member of the Leicester FA.

2. The charge was heard by three men who had no jurisdiction to hear it. The rules of the county FA give jurisdiction to the whole council of the county FA, and there was no power to delegate.

On this Lord Denning commented:

> I quite appreciate Mr Sparrow's submission that these are difficult points of law on which there are authorities to be cited and rules to be construed. So much so that I do not think the FA is itself a suitable body to decide them. It would be much better, I should think, for the club to bring these points straight away before the court in an action for a declaration. That is a course which they are perfectly entitled to take at once before the appeal is heard by the FA.... As Romer L.J. said in *Lee* v *Showmen's Guild of Great Britain*:[1] 'The proper tribunals for the determination of legal disputes in this country are the courts, and they are the only tribunals which, by training and experience, and assisted by properly qualified advocates, are fitted for the task.'
>
> Although it is open to the club to come to the court to decide the points, they have not done so. They are sticking to their appeal to the FA. They ask that the points be decided by that body. They want to have counsel and solicitor to argue them before the FA. The FA decline.

Ultimately, all three members of the Court of Appeal decided that Rule 38(b), excluding legal representation, was not, in itself, contrary to natural justice. Lord Denning thought, however, that exclusion was a matter of discretion, and that there could well be circumstances in which it was wise to allow it. He doubted, in fact, whether it was competent for a voluntary association to make an absolute rule excluding legal representation. Obviously, this question will arise again at a later date.

There was, however, a second question. Rule 40(b) of the FA's rules provides: 'The rules of the association are sufficient

---

[1] [1952] 2 Q.B. 329, 354.

to enable the council as the governing authority to deal with all cases of dispute, and legal proceedings shall only be taken as a last resort, and then only with the consent of the council.'

This, it will be seen, is in a form similar to the Scottish rule, and as Lord Kilbrandon had already done, Lord Denning made short work of it. 'If that rule were valid, it would prevent the club from bringing any action in the courts without the consent of the council. But the rule is plainly invalid.'

It is indeed surprising that it has survived so long.

The Player's Contract of Service

The changes in the structure of football, and in the rewards which a professional footballer now receives, were discussed in general terms in Chapter Two. The present chapter will be concerned more closely with the nature of football as a career.

Under favourable conditions, a playing career may extend over twenty years. When he retires, the player will still be, in modern eyes, a young man, and accordingly, all major professional clubs today give increasing attention to educational schemes which aim to train a player for an occupation when his playing days are at an end.

Although there are brilliant exceptions who enter the professional game at a later age, most players who are highly successful will have been attracted to a club by the time they are fifteen, and today they would become apprentices. The search for schoolboys who are likely to make the grade in professional football is most extensive, but much of it concentrates upon players who appear in schoolboy internationals, and other representative matches. Here, once again, it is evident that the big clubs are in the most favourable position. Their scouting organisations are the most developed and the boy himself is likely to be more eager to join a club with a distinguished tradition, and which possesses a ground with extensive training facilities.

The position of apprentices is regulated by Rule 12 of the rules of the Football Association, and by Regulation 47 of the Football League, which is supplementary to it. Apprenticeship extends over two or three years, ie, between the apprentice's fifteenth and seventeenth or eighteenth birthdays. At seventeen, the apprentice may sign professional forms for his club. If he does not, the apprenticeship continues until the eighteenth birthday, when the apprentice must finally decide whether to sign professional forms, or revert to his status as an amateur. The club where he has served his apprenticeship has the first right to his signature as a professional. If it does not wish to register him, the apprentice may then look elsewhere.

Every apprentice must be registered with the Football Association by means of completing Form G (3), and he may not play for his club until this form has been completed. He may apply to his club at any time for cancellation of his registration, and in this event he reverts at once to amateur status. If he chooses to end his apprenticeship in this way he cannot sign a registration form or play for a professional club until after a lapse of two years, unless the club for which he was registered as an apprentice agrees. If the apprentice or his parents request it, the club must allow him to continue his education or take suitable vocational training during his apprenticeship.

The contract contained in Form G (3) provides that if the club fails to fulfil the condition of the contract in respect of his training, the apprentice shall be entitled to apply to his club for cancellation of his registration and contract of service, and either revert to his amateur status or sign as an apprentice for another club. He has a right to appeal to the Football League if his application is unreasonably refused or delayed, and there is a further right of appeal to the Football Association. During apprenticeship there is a minimum wage of £5 a week, and a maximum of £7 between 15 and 16, or £8 between 16 and 17, and £10 between 17 and 18.

The process whereby a player is registered as a full professional for a club is a complicated one. The player completes a form, known as Form G (2), stating that he agrees to play for the registering club, and also undertaking to observe the rules, regulations and bye-laws of the Football Association. The secretary of the club also signs a form certifying that he has signed the player. These forms, together with a completed form of agreement, are in standard form, supplied by the Football Association. No other form of agreement is recognised. It sets out the terms and conditions of employment, and in particular it contains the option for renewal which has already been discussed. The option is for a period which is not longer than the original period of employment, and is on terms and conditions not less favourable than those which applied during the original period. It must be exercised by the club before the last day of the playing season in which the original contract terminates.

The present arrangement governing contracts of service was worked out between the Football League, the Football Association and the Professional Footballers' Association after extended discussions, and if the rules of the League and the Football Association are studied, it will be apparent that today the players' interests have been fully protected.

When a club wishes to exercise its option, it gives notice in writing to the player, and the notice must specify the terms and conditions offered during the renewal period. The player has the right within twenty-eight days of the offer to reply in writing to the club, stating that he does not accept the terms offered. The club now has a choice of courses of action. It can negotiate with the player, in the hope of finding terms acceptable to both club and player; it can agree to transfer the player; or, thirdly, either party may refer their dispute to the management committee of the League. If either party is dissatisfied with the League's decision, there is a further appeal, to be made within twenty-eight days of the decision, to the League's appeals committee. Should the player's original contract expire whilst this procedure is in operation, it is regarded as continuing until the final decision of the appeals committee is given.

All these matters are set out in full in the player's contract, together with a number of other matters, particularly those relating to discipline and training, and the power of the club to suspend a player for misconduct or breaches of discipline. The suspension may not exceed fourteen days, and the club has also power to fine a player not more than two weeks' wages. Any fine or suspension must be promptly notified to the Football Association, to whom also the players may appeal.

Another necessary provision in the player's contract sets out the procedure for cancelling a player's contract, and also the player's right of appeal to the league in which the club plays. When a club notifies a player that his agreement is being terminated, it must at the same time state the reasons for this action, and it must also inform the league, to whom the player may appeal within seven days. When the league management committee (or the appeals committee) have decided the matter, it must be reported to the Football Association, and (where this is the league's decision) the player's contract and his registration are cancelled.

All these matters relating to the player's contract are set out in the rules of the Football Association. The Football League also requires the player to be registered, and it also requires his club to supply the League with a copy of his contract of service.

Sometimes a player's registration is cancelled, or he is released by his club on the ground of permanent disability. In such a case he may not be registered for another club without the consent of the club for which he was last registered. Regulation 50 adds: 'Any professional player who has applied for and been paid the amount standing to his credit in the Provident Fund or who has received the Permanent Total Disablement Payment from the Football League Personal Account Insurance Scheme shall not be registered for any club.'

The Players' Union also have an insurance scheme against disablement for their members. In *Alder* v *Moore*,[1] Moore was a professional player who had been seriously injured in play, and had been advised that he would never be able to play again. He was nominated by the Association Football Players' and Trainers' Union to be a beneficiary under a policy of insurance taken out by them in favour of any member of the union registered as a player with the Football League. He therefore received £500 in payment for total disablement, agreeing at the same time that if he played again, he would refund the £500. Moore subsequently

---

[1] [1960] Current Law 386.

became a part-time professional with a non-League club, and the underwriters sued for the return of the £500. The Court of Appeal held (by a majority) that the £500 was recoverable, and they rejected the argument that the sum was only repayable if the player signed for another League club.

By Regulation 53 of the Football League, the terms and conditions of all transfers must be notified to the management committee, and all transfers require its approval. Usually there is no problem, but the regulation states: 'There shall be no fixed maximum transfer fee, but no transfer shall be registered until the management committee are satisfied that an appropriate fee has been paid, or its payment adequately secured.'

Matters relating to the player's contract have sometimes reached the courts in recent years. Frequently, one of the conditions which the player makes on agreeing to a transfer is that the club should provide him with a house, preferably near the club headquarters. Naturally, when his agreement terminates, he must vacate it. In *Bournemouth and Boscombe Athletic FC v Stephens*,[1] Stephens, a professional player for Bournemouth, rented a flat from the club. Owing to ill-health, his contract was terminated and the club sought to regain possession of the flat in order to let it to another player. The club brought an action in the county court, and the judge, holding that a professional footballer's employment is whole-time, therefore made an order permitting the club to regain possession of the flat.

At one time, it was customary for the player's contract to contain provisions specifying summer wages at lower rates than during the playing season. The extension of the playing season and summer tours have led to a different system, but the case of *Inland Revenue Commissioners v Albion Rovers FC*[2] produced an important decision of the House of Lords on the nature of summer wages. The case, a highly complicated one, arose out of the change in players' contracts, so that they ran from 1 August to 31 July, instead of from 1 May to 30 April, as hitherto. The

---

[1] [1951] 102 L.J. 52.   [2] [1952] 45 R. & I.T. 505.

problem to be decided was the determination of the tax-year against which players' summer wages could be placed. The House of Lords decided that the wages paid in the summer of 1949 were not an expense in the nature of a bonus, attached to the 1948-49 season, but were really attributable to the forthcoming season, for which the training was being undertaken.

A matter which is conspicuously absent from both the rules of the Football Association and the regulations of the Football League is any statement upon the *amount* of wages or the bonuses payable for success in the various competitions for which the clubs may have entered, or for television or broadcasting rights, or other payments to which the player may be entitled. Their current practice is in sharp contrast to that which existed until the abolition of the maximum wage. Until then the extent to which a club could reward its players was fenced in by restictive provisions, and penalties were sometimes imposed on clubs for straying outside the permitted limits. Today a totally different attitude prevails, and the contract is regarded as primarily a matter between the player and his club, although one feature of the old system survives. A player must deal directly with the club on signing, renewal of the contract, or transfer. Neither Football Association nor League permit the intervention of any agent, although there is nothing to prevent a player from consulting the secretary of the Players' Union, if he chooses. Contracts are individual, even between players of the same club, and today the varying rates of pay arouse no more comment than those paid to television and theatrical performers. The fears that such variations would affect the club's performances have proved quite unfounded. What it has done is to make the bargaining between player and club a much tougher and prolonged business than formerly, and it is probable that more transfers are requested by players because they feel they are entitled to higher wages than the club has offered them than for any other reason. This, in turn, has greatly increased the manager's burden in retaining a happy and successful club.

One wonders what some of the great players of the past—the

Tom Lawtons, the Wilf Mannions and even the Tom Finneys—
make of this glittering new world. In their day they occupied the
headlines as much, or even more extensively, but their rewards
were extremely modest by comparison. Indeed, it could be
strongly argued that the professional footballer is in a stronger
position than a popular entertainer. His active career is at least
as long, and his employment is all the year round. There are
dangers, however, even in the adulation which the player attracts.
Today, the leading player may live in a fashionable suburb, and
run two smart cars. His companions are often drawn from the
world of entertainment. Certainly the link with it is much closer
than it used to be. Behind this colourful life, behind the nightclub and the fashionable restaurants and lively parties, is the
basic condition of a professional footballer's career—the necessity
to keep fit. Only managers are fully aware what a continuing
problem this is, or how much the team as a whole suffers if a
little slackness creeps in. Occasionally, however, suspension of a
player, and paragraphs in the popular press detailing incidents in
which players had been involved, hint at the existence of a new
problem which the high incomes of the present-day have created
—the problem of the 'with-it' young player who is unable to
keep his feet firmly on the ground. Once again, it would seem
that English players have come somewhat late to this fashionable
life. Their counterparts in Italy and South America have been
the spoilt children of a cosmopolitan society a good deal longer;
but already one or two outstanding players in England have
shown signs of succumbing to good living and excessive adulation in the mass media; although, taken as a whole, the English
professional players have adjusted well to the changed social environment into which their high rewards have brought them.

One final observation may be made. The players, equally with
the public, should have an interest in maintaining the nation-
wide character of professional football. If it ever dwindled to a
small group of clubs, as baseball has done in the United States,
it would lose its hold on public interest and it could then only
support a handful of players. The full-time player in a struggling

club in a small provincial town has his place, as well as the international star. Even if the conclusion is stated in its lowest terms, the more clubs that can exist, the more managerial places there are to be filled when playing days are done.

II

Some Present Problems

In the preceding chapters a number of problems affecting the organisation of football at the present time have been mentioned. Possibly the most important of all is the relation of those who govern football with the media of communication, and especially with the daily press and television. This can be defined as a love-hate relationship. Each is essential to the other. League football, and all that results from it, is news. Not infrequently, and especially when players and managers change clubs unexpectedly, it is sensational news, which is presented with up-to-the-minute coverage, and where possible by means of interviews with the protagonists. Accuracy of prediction, a suggestion of inside knowledge, and outspoken criticism stimulate sales of newspapers. It is not open to question that the coverage given to racing and football affect circulation to a greater extent than the political views which a newspaper may express. It is equally true that the attention paid by the press is the life-blood of league football. Without it, interest would flag, and if the activities of all concerned were not presented dramatically, attendances would dwindle. Today, also, there is a third major factor in the almost universal addiction to football pools. Analysis of form and of systems of forecasting stimulate newspaper sales and extend interest in the game itself.

On the other hand both the Football League and the Football Association not infrequently give the impression that they resent the criticisms which sports writers in the daily press so often offer. It cannot be denied that a good deal of it is purely ephemeral, designed rather to focus attention upon a particular incident or person, than to make a constructive contribution to the future well-being of the game. On the other hand, those who control football sometimes show a surprising lack of familiarity with the methods which popular newspapers use to elicit information. If government departments and large firms have found it prudent to appoint high-calibre public relations officers, and in this way to reduce pressure upon leading politicians and business men, the football world might find it useful to follow suit. Modern publicity is concerned with the 'image', and it is not open to question that the 'image' of football administrators is capable of a good deal of improvement.

One complication at the present time is the readiness of professional footballers to capitalise on their news value, either by way of interviews or by press notices. So far as written contributions are concerned, the League seeks to exercise a certain amount of control. Regulation 74 provides:

> All clubs must incorporate in any Agreements with their employees an undertaking on the part of the employee to seek the permission of the Club before contributing to the Press, Television or Radio. It is the responsibility of the Club to ensure that any permission so granted is not used by the employee in such a way as to bring the League or any Club into disrepute.

The intention of the regulation is quite clear, and most footballers observe the spirit of it, as well as the letter, but there have been instances where the damage done, not only to a club but to the player himself, has far outweighed any benefit received; and this is even more true of interviews. A statement by Jeff Astle, the international centre-forward of West Bromwich Albion, that he had sold Cup Final tickets allotted to him in 1968 by the club at a profit of £200 resulted in his appearance before an FA commission, which imposed both a fine of £200 and a permanent ban on the allotment of such tickets to him in the future. An unfortunate admission by Jack Charlton of Leeds United that there were players he would 'do' for rough play, has brought him into unmerited disfavour. It is not only football directors or officials who show lack of finesse when dealing with the press.

There is yet another complicating factor—the player of outstanding reputation who has recently retired from the game and who receives a contract to write for a period for the daily or weekly press. Their contributions are eagerly read as likely to lift the veil on what really happens in football. Unfortunately, such contributions do not possess continuing appeal, either to the public or to the employing newspaper, unless they contain a substantial quota of sensational incidents, which often undergo considerable embellishment in being prepared for publication. Only too often directors appear in such contributions as motivated by ignorance of the game or worse. Obviously the writers in most cases have no knowledge of board-room difficulties, and there is little recognition of the years of service without financial reward.

Television has introduced a technique which has provoked another adverse reaction from the Football League and the Football Association. This is the 'slow-action' play-back of some incident in the game, followed by the comments of players, managers, and possibly others upon the episode. There have recently been several such episodes, more than one of which concerned off-side decisions of referees, in which those decisions were sharply criticised. As might have been expected, both organisations condemned this practice, and from the standpoint of the game as a whole such condemnation is entirely justified. Referees would not be human if they did not make occasional mistakes, as even judges have been known to do, but if the finality of their decisions upon the playing of the game itself can be called into question by a television panel, their authority upon the field would be most seriously prejudiced.

It is frequently suggested that today there is too much football and that the playing season is too long. As a result of a decision of the Football Association, taken at the end of the 1970-71 season, football may now be played in every month of the year except July when, presumably, both players and administrators need a holiday. When the playing season was first established it was much shorter, and since many of the early players were often cricketers of note, there was for some time an assumption that the football season and the cricket season only slightly overlapped. As a result of this arrangement, the Cup Final on the first Saturday in May ended the season for all major competitions, leaving only a few charity matches to be played. Thereafter, there was a break until the third Saturday in August, when the county championship matches were drawing to a close.

A number of things have happened in recent years to change this picture. One has been the decline in interest in cricket generally, and in the county championship in particular. It can no longer be argued that attendances at county matches will suffer from competition with football. The attendances are no longer there, and the county championship itself only survives in a modified form, and interest in it is so tepid that even the efforts of the press fail to improve the response of the public. One matter which has received too little attention in connection with cricket is the climatic pattern of the past two hundred years. First-class cricket had its origin in eighteenth-century country-house matches, played under almost perfect conditions. Was there a long succession of fine, warm summers in the second half of the eighteenth century? The spread of the game would seem to suggest it. We know that there was a succession of long, fine summers in the last quarter of the nineteenth century, when county cricket reached the peak of its popularity. The pattern is so different today that watching a day's cricket in comfort has become little more than a memory. There are, however, other reasons for the disappearance of cricket crowds. One is the pace of modern industrial life, making the possibility of watching a substantial part of a county match remote. Another is the negative character of much county cricket. The contrast in the rate of run-getting is notable. Yorkshire once scored 880 runs in an innings against Warwickshire. That is, in itself, remarkable, but there are two other noteworthy features about this score. The first is that Yorkshire should have found it necessary to make so many runs. The second is that the match was finished. And how long is it since any batsman made a century before lunch? A scoring rate of two or three runs an over will never be popular,

L

and it is significant that there is widespread support of one-day Sunday cricket.

Competition with cricket for public support is therefore no longer a problem. There is another important reason for the change. The player is now a whole-time player. He is not engaged for a playing season at one rate of pay, and then placed on much reduced summer wages as he used to be. Today he is much more expensive, and therefore clubs expect a great deal more from him. Further, he is now trained to a higher pitch of physical fitness, and accordingly a balance must be struck between staleness and idleness. As a result, he has come to enjoy a holiday comparable with that of other skilled men, but no longer.

But what about the reaction of the public to the longer season? Can interest be sustained at the required pitch over so long a period? The obvious reply to this is that it will make very little practical difference. So long as the clash for the Cup Final remains what it is, practically all League fixtures will be completed at that time, and clubs will be ready to undertake foreign tours. There is no suggestion that more fixtures should be crowded into a season which is already full. In the long run, it may be that the extension benefits amateur clubs most. Since only a small number of them possess lights good enough to play a match under, the programmes of amateur leagues frequently have to be completed by the desperate expedient of playing almost every evening at the end of the season. This is almost inescapable where an amateur club has had one or more lengthy cup runs, for in their case again cup-ties and replays can only be completed on Saturdays. So long as amateur leagues resist the temptation to increase their size, end-of-season fixtures will be less of a nightmare. On the other hand, they are not welcomed by the officials of amateur leagues, who have already found the close season too short a time in which to finish the business of one season and undertake the preparation for the next.

There is no suggestion that the latest extension of the season should be accompanied by an interruption in the season, to extend over three or four weeks in January or February. This suggestion has only to be stated for its impractability to be apparent. It is prompted, of course, by the recognition that the weather is usually at its worst at that time. But there is no certainty of this. Some winters, and more especially in the south of England, are so mild that any interruption is quite unnecessary. Even in a hard winter, the time of its incidence is uncertain. On the other hand, an interruption of the League programme, and a postponement of one or more rounds of the Cup, would provoke irritation among football supporters (and would interrupt the pools); and again, amateur football would be seriously affected. On the whole, the present system of cancelling games only when conditions are shown to be impossible seems to work satisfactorily.

Those who have made suggestions of this kind have sometimes suggested also that we have too much football, and that the public interest would be more strongly sustained if there were less of it. It is difficult to see upon what evidence such a suggestion is founded. Attendances flag for clearly ascertainable reasons—bad weather, large-scale local unemployment, and indifferent performances of the club supported. Where these factors are not present, support is usually fairly steady throughout the season, rising during a cup run or where the club is battling strongly for promotion. The chief value of the close season is that it marks the end of one campaign and the beginning of the next. As the fixtures are completed towards the end of the season, hopes and fears are fully realised, and clubs begin to take stock of their needs for the following season. Exactly the same situation existed when the season was shorter. Its extension does not appear to have changed things noticeably. It has not really affected the position of supporters, for there will be very little change in the arrangement of fixtures. What may occur is that clubs will play one or two more matches outside the League structure, although unless these are played against fairly well-known clubs from abroad they will not attract support in great numbers.

A quite distinct question which is often asked is: Do we have too many League clubs? To some extent the argument that there are too many is self-defeating, for the clubs are there, whether they are in membership with the League or not, and not infrequently professional non-League clubs give League members —even some of the most distinguished of them—a rude shock.

There have been suggestions that the divisions of the League should be reduced in number—to three, or even to two; or alternatively that the number of clubs in each division should be reduced. It is difficult to see any force in the second suggestion. All League clubs now possess lighting installations, and they do not experience any difficulty in completing their fixtures. Under modern conditions, the question of congestion of fixtures can only arise where a club has had a number of games in several cup competitions—a situation which was responsible for Leeds United failing to win any honour in the 1969-70 season. In the following season, however, the Arsenal, with a heavy programme, were more successful, winning both English trophies, but failing in their European Cup competition. If there is congestion today, it is only in respect of the fixtures of one or two very successful clubs (which usually possess great reserve strength) and it is primarily the result of 'going into Europe'. Since this is an extremely profitable enterprise both for the club and players, too much sympathy should not be expended on them if all their ambitions are not realised.

There can only be one conclusion about the effect of the present League structure upon the clubs themselves. The knowledge that great clubs such as Aston Villa, Preston North End, Blackburn Rovers, Bolton Wanderers and Fulham can tumble from the First to the Third Division in the course of one or two seasons has the effect of increasing the competition between clubs for survival. Perhaps those clubs might temporarily have wished that the League had been limited to two divisions, for it is difficult to believe that any of them would have failed to secure re-election. The inclusion of no less than ninety-two clubs ensures that the League is truly national, and that within that group of ninety-two there is sufficient variety in the composition of the divisions to ensure that the annual competition has some novelty.

Perhaps the point in the structure where criticism can be most strongly directed is at the bottom of the Fourth Division, where re-election, rather than new admissions, is the rule. The reasons for this have been mentioned in an earlier chapter, and under the present system it is fully understandable that a League club should do its utmost to retain its League status. The suggestion has already been made that the burden of the Fourth Division clubs would be eased if the division were divided into northern and southern sections. This would involve taking in some of the ambitious non-League clubs who knock so regularly on the League door. Some of them have grounds and organisations which compare favourably with those of a number of Fourth Division clubs.

The situation would be still further improved if, along with such a rearrangement of the Fourth Division, there were introduced a practice whereby the bottom club, or bottom two clubs in each section, exchanged places with the strongest professional non-League clubs in the area. In the south, this would be the champion club of the Southern League, and possibly the runner-up. This suggestion is not new. It has been put forward on a number of occasions by the Southern League and has been rejected by the Football League. It would strengthen competition between Fourth Division clubs, and further, the loss of status of a club going out of the League would not be permanent as it is today. Reorganisation and a successful season in another league could bring it back into the Football League.

There is another reason why this suggestion ought to be considered further. Under the agreement between the Football Association and the Football League, mentioned in Chapter Seven, the Association, for practical purposes, handed over the interests of professional football to the League. The League, however, has done nothing at all for the non-League clubs. It is doubtful whether it is even conscious of the existence of many of them. Yet the Southern League—to give only one example—has loyally supported the efforts of its strongest members to obtain admission to the Football League, and in 1920 the entire membership of the Southern League became the Third Division (not yet Southern Section). Each time the Southern League has lost its strongest members to the Football League, it has recruited with quite remarkable success.

Referees are not so much a problem as a centre of discussion. Their position is anomalous and their independence is jealously guarded. If it were seriously threatened, they could not continue to function and the game itself would be in danger of falling into disrepute. All referees give their services because they are enthusiasts for the game. They keep in training and travel long distances for fees which today are quite nominal. The present fee for refereeing a Football League match is £10.50. A League linesman receives exactly half this amount, and there is a fixed scale of expenses. One item throws a sharp light upon the conditions under which they act: 'An official who has to leave home before 8.0 am, or who cannot complete his return journey before midnight on the day of a match shall be entitled to claim an additional £1.' Referees of lesser senior leagues receive no more than £2 to £5 a match, yet it is essential they should be of good quality.

Much time and work goes into the training of referees, both by the referee himself and by his county association. The referees themselves have a county organisation, which is subdivided into local divisions. At the divisional meeting there is frequently instruction in the art of refereeing, and almost invariably there is discussion of particular problems. A man who wishes to become a referee applies to his local secretary, and he begins as a linesman. His proficiency will be assessed by his local referees' association, by the leagues in which he officiates, and by the referees' committee of the county association. He will also be required to pass examinations. If successful, he will progress from Class III, by way of Class II, to Class I, from which the county will select referees to handle the most important games in the county programme, and also to send on to the Football League, and other major leagues, for inclusion on their lists.

In general, a referee gives up when he is between forty and forty-five years old, for his job is almost as taxing physically as a player's. Although referees are drawn from all ranks, and may include clergymen, members of the services (and particularly of the RAF), bank managers, and workers of every kind, there is no doubt that the most influential group in their ranks are school teachers, possibly because there is no doubt that they will be able to fulfil their commitments. A few players from time to time turn to refereeing, but in general it seems to have no great attraction for them. As the seasons pass, the search for good young referees becomes keener, for it is unfortunately true that the decline in the numbers of persons willing to serve on the committees of amateur football clubs is matched by the decline in the number of aspirants to referee. This problem is constantly present to county associations, who have particular difficulty in meeting the demand for linesmen. Some leagues of lesser rank have already had to abandon the attempt to provide neutral linesmen, and have been compelled to leave it to the competing clubs to provide them.

Up to the present time, the League has resisted the suggestion that it should appoint professional referees at a salary far in excess of the small fees now paid. It might be that an absence of sufficient referees of the necessary standard may compel the League to take such a course, although even then there is no guarantee that debatable results would be avoided. Football is not like horse-racing, where the camera is used to determine close finishes. The referee must make split-second decisions. The remarkable thing is that good referees make so very few mistakes, although it is usually forgotten that referees, like players, have good games and bad games. When they have bad games, they are as conscious of it as the players are.

One problem which in recent years has continued to attract attention has been the status and tenure of the manager of a League club—or indeed to a lesser degree of any professional club. It has already been pointed out that the salaries of managers have kept pace with those of the players. A successful manager may earn as much as £10,000 a year with liberal expenses—and many players keep their eyes firmly fixed upon a managerial post when their playing careers are drawing to an end. Indeed, it is frequently the case that a player retires earlier than he would otherwise have done in order to become a manager. There are many attractions, but there are also penalties. A manager, under modern cut-throat conditions, is judged solely on his capacity to bring success to the club. Looked at broadly, this is absurd. The League competition is designed expressly to ensure that some clubs are successful, and that some are not. Further, failure may have nothing to do with the manager, even remotely. It may be the result of a run of injuries, or some other cause. None of these things count in the day of reckoning, ie, at the end of a season in which the club has dropped a division. At such a time, the fact that the manager has a contract with several years to run will make no difference. In the hope of doing better next season, the manager will be compensated and his successor appointed. Probably, too, the players in whom the manager had faith, or some of them, will be placed on the open-to-transfer list.

The turnover in managers is so great that the indefatigable Mr Clive Jenkins has suggested that they should join the swollen ranks of his own union. It is difficult to believe that they would accede. The application of union rules to some managerial activities might not be a bad thing, but the managers themselves would not welcome it.

Looked at in detachment, the present managerial problem is almost insoluble, and it may be that many managers would not wish for a solution, at any rate if it would restrict their activities. Many of them may suffer from ulcers, caused by the stress of a long season, but few quit on that account, and of those who temporarily withdraw, most return. Since many managers are ex-players, they are not strangers to the hazards of being dropped for lack of form. As a manager, the same procedure is continued in a rather different idiom.

It has already been pointed out that the rise of the modern race of managers has resulted in the almost total dissociation of the board of directors from the players—although, so far as the public and the press are concerned, if things go wrong it is the directors who are responsible. And so they are, and if they so decide they can take action in the only way now open to them. They can fire the manager. Managers themselves fully understand that the almost absolute authority which they now have is accompanied by complete responsibility for the club's performances on the playing field, and also the risk of dismissal for failure.

At the same time, increased competitiveness among clubs for the reputedly successful manager, who can turn failure into success in the shortest possible space of time, is producing new antagonisms and conflicts which are certainly not good for the game as a whole. The turnover in managers tends to reach a climax just before the end of a season when prospects of relegation intensify, and just after the end of a season when clubs are considering the next campaign. Almost every modern manager knows that his continuance in office depends upon the success of his team, and this in turn depends on the extent to which his players have confidence in his judgment.

It takes no considerable thought to realise that this strengthens the will to win, not always in the most gentlemanly way, and that, to use the euphemism beloved by club managers on television, the game has become more 'physical'. The chief responsibility for this rests upon the manager and his staff. Their job is to select and train teams that will win matches, and so long as a player is not sent off (with the strong probability that he will be suspended from playing for a time), his methods of achieving success will not be too closely scrutinised.

This is, of course, only one aspect of modern play. There is a great deal more. There are speed, precision, and the individual skill which, in a really great player, can never be reduced to a pattern, and which will always prove attractive to crowds. Further, it is probable that there are no more fouls in a first-class game today than there were forty, fifty or even more years ago. The Corinthians were always noted for the robustness of their play, as were the Wanderers before them. There is, however, an important difference between the foul that is the product of enthusiasm and imperfect physical control, and the deliberate fouls from which it is intended to derive a playing advantage. Sometimes it is suggested by the press that directors, or even managers, should 'give a lead' in stamping out foul play. Since both are animated by the same determination that the club should be successful, it is not surprising that these appeals meet with little response. Nevertheless, the dangers of permitting present tendencies to develop are clearly shown in the football played in South America. Finally, it is the case that rough play in the field is a frequent cause of violence on the terraces.

Perhaps the most serious problem needing consideration is the decline of the amateur game. Because there are still a large number of leagues and competitions and a considerable number of people play each week-end, the extent of that decline is not fully appreciated. The reasons for it are numerous and varied. One which should be placed high on the list is the mobility of young people as compared with the lives of their parents and grandparents. Mobility should be understood in a double sense. A player may change jobs and leave an area. Even if he does not, marriage and the acquisition of a car frequently ends his serious football. Today, when the wife has a job as well as the husband, the week-end is prized and is given up to activities which both can share.

One other reason for the decline of amateur football is the fact that in an increasing number of schools it has been replaced by Rugby. It is very hard to understand this. Whilst first-class Rugby football is a game in which skill and physical courage are blended, the game as played at many schools has little but honest endeavour to commend it. Association football is learned more easily, and, as the schoolboy international games show, it is capable of being played at the very highest standard by schoolboys.

There are in addition other reasons for the decline, some of which have been mentioned earlier. It is becoming more difficult and more expensive to keep a senior amateur club in being year

by year. Rates, which in the past were usually negligible, have
become an important item. Planning improvements is a long and
also an expensive process, even though most local councils tend
to react in a helpful way to football clubs. The cost of recurrent
domestic items—travelling, laundering, equipment and administration—rises annually faster than income. Some clubs have
already disappeared. Others may follow in the near future. Others
again are dropping out of the amateur ranks altogether, and are
becoming professional clubs. At the end of the 1970-71 season,
Skelmersdale United became a professional organisation, immediately after winning the Amateur Cup. At the same time, Weald-
stone and other clubs left the Isthmian League to become professional clubs and to join the extended Southern League. The
drift away from the Isthmian League, once the acknowledged
premier amateur league in the south, is especially significant.
In recent years, a group of clubs have evidently found the annual
league competition unattractive, as their support has dwindled.
Indeed, one of the most serious criticisms which can be made of
some leading amateur competitions is that they are unprogressive.
Existing as closed corporations, they seem to have little interest in
football outside the narrow circle of their membership, which
tends to remain stable over long periods. A short time ago the
Football Association attempted to stimulate a movement towards
more comprehensive senior amateur football, with regional
leagues operating in several divisions. The Athenian League extended its organisation and its area of operations in conformity
with this policy, but others have failed to follow this example
and their standard of play is suffering in consequence. Obviously
they cannot hope to compete for the limited support which is now
available outside the Football League with progressive professional competitions such as the Southern League. It begins to look
as if senior amateur football can only survive when either it is
closely integrated with social activities which are conducted
profitably, or when it is linked with some large firm. There are,
of course, a considerable number of football clubs associated with
firms, but many of them have found recently that the firm has

been a good deal less ready to support them than it had been in easier times. In any case, football is merely one of the sports for which a works social club is organised, and it has many competitors for available funds.

There is still another factor which is affecting the survival of many of our senior amateur clubs and the competitions in which they play. Now that Sunday football is within the jurisdiction of the Football Association, it has been organised on a most comprehensive scale, and although for the most part it is played on public recreation grounds, it attracts large crowds on Sunday mornings. The majority of the players will also be members of clubs who play on Saturday, and unfortunately it is far from rare for a player to regard his Sunday game as the one of primary importance.

The plight of senior amateur football in England is therefore serious, but it is not yet desperate. It would be most unfortunate if the amateur game were to disintegrate into local junior football and the Sunday game. Even the Football League could not be indifferent to such a collapse, for senior amateur football is one recruiting ground, though a less important one than it used to be.

The root of the trouble is that much senior amateur football has become an embarrassing hybrid. It is not professional, and it is not run on the business lines of a professional club; but it is not amateur football in the old sense, either; its major activities are conducted for the purpose of meeting bills which grow steadily larger, and in which the provision of players' 'expenses', often by the most circuitous of routes, is a constant nightmare. For this reason, a very large number of people are holding back from participation. In their view the effort is not worth while.

The prospect for the future of amateur football is not a hopeful one. Can anything be done to improve it? Some attempts have been made from time to time, but without altering the picture significantly. One possibility would be to reorganise it on county and regional lines, thereby rationalising the functions of the leagues and eliminating overlapping. To do this would be to make serious inroads on the autonomy of leagues, which they greatly prize. Since there are already too few persons willing to come forward to give effective service at county level, it would only be a first step towards a regional organisation in which promotion and relegation had a place. Even if this were done, it is doubtful whether it would have the effect of bringing the crowds back. It may be that the day of amateur football as an entertainment has already passed. It may also be that there will be more defections to the ranks of the non-League professional clubs, where at least some steps towards reorganisation on a national basis have been taken.

For amateur football which is truly amateur there will always be a place, just as there is a place for Rugby Union football. This, however, is remote from the highly competitive and semi-commercial activities of the better-known senior amateur clubs. If the latter activities are to survive in their present condition, it is because they are firmly linked with a wide range of other activities which return a substantial profit. Perhaps it is in the stimulation of developments of this kind that the national organisations could most usefully play a part. So also could local authorities, by making a ready response to planning applications for necessary developments.

At this point in time it is nevertheless valuable to ask whether so much effort in the sphere of organisation and fund-raising is justified by the results? Why, if fewer and fewer people come to watch amateur games, should the attempt be made to meet the ever-increasing expenses of playing the game? Helping eleven, or twenty-two young athletes to play a game of football is one thing; maintaining a senior amateur club is something altogether different. Put in this way, the dilemma is at once apparent. Senior amateur football has become a hybrid, and it may be questioned whether today there is any considerable value in troubling about the status of players, except in the clubs which are demonstrably amateur, in which the player does not receive any expenses at all. This would imply that, outside the ranks of the Amateur Football Association, the whole question of expenses should cease to be the concern of the county and national associations. Proposals of this kind have been made in the past, but they have been strongly resisted, primarily on the ground that it would no longer be possible to select representative sides for international games, and for the Olympic Games. It is for this reason that the apparently rigid rules of the Football Association governing payments for expenses have been drawn, and why the Football Association is making a last effort to enforce them by obtaining from players selected for representative matches a signed declaration that they have received only permissible expenses.

This is, nevertheless, no more than one special problem within a much bigger one. If one looks at senior amateur football in detachment, one is compelled to admit that its hold upon public attention has diminished steadily in the last two decades, and that it is likely to shrink still further in the future. The number of players who are prepared to submit to its discipline, in spite of the attractions of other sports and pastimes, is getting fewer year by year. So far as the public is concerned, the attractions of the sports programmes on television have certainly hit the amateurs more than they have affected the professional game. In addition, tastes in sport have changed. Motor racing draws large crowds, whilst some racecourses and amateur football grounds are largely deserted. Even athletics are today more popular. Still more serious is the fact that, except where amateur clubs have been reorganised around what are, in substance, social centres, they have increasing difficulty in finding public-spirited men who will undertake, on a voluntary basis, the work of organisation which must be done if the club is to function efficiently. In this respect football clubs are repeating the experiences of many other social groups, including nonconformist churches and friendly societies. Many reasons for this decline in voluntary public service might be suggested. Perhaps the most important is the general assumption that it can achieve little in face of the ever-more comprehensive pattern of activities initiated, regulated or supported by the state. This assumption has been strengthened by the institution of a minister responsible for the encouragement of sport and physical recreation. Today, it would seem, these require stimulation, organisation and ultimately support from public funds in the same way that a large number of other social activities do. They may even require the institution of a number of local officers for sport and physical recreation, who in turn will act in association with local committees. Admirable as such developments might be, they will once again have the effect of drawing away from amateur clubs persons whose services would be badly needed.

Regretfully one is compelled to conclude that the ideals of those who created Association football over a century ago are today only dimly perceived. On the one side, there has been developed the professional game as a major entertainment in which stars directly comparable with those of the cinema and television receive high rewards and enjoy a vast following. On the other side is the complex organisation of amateur football, divided again between those who continue to regard a game of football as a healthy Saturday afternoon occupation, and others who bring to it skill and training, but who expect to receive not-inconsiderable expenses for so doing. There can be little doubt that the former group will survive. It does not depend on public support, and it is largely indifferent to the presence or absence of spectators. The second group is facing increasing difficulty in its efforts to survive. It is losing some of its best-known clubs to the ranks of the professional leagues, and it has failed to reorganise its league structure in such a way as to reawaken public interest in its competitions. With increasing expenses, vanishing support, and a shortage of persons willing to serve on its committees, the future for them is bleak.

12

Violence - On and Off the Field

Violence today is such a major problem—not by any means in football alone—that it requires separate discussion. Football has been affected by two distinct manifestations. What is not at present clear is the extent to which they are linked.

The season 1971-72 opened sensationally. By half-time on the first Saturday, a whole group of League players had been 'booked'. As the season progressed the number rose rapidly, and bookings were headline news. Naturally, reactions were extremely varied, and in some instances entirely predictable. It quickly emerged that before the end of the previous season, referees and representatives of the Football Association administration and of the management committee of the Football League had met in secret conclave to devise a fresh set of instructions for League referees (and, by implication, for other referees also), aimed at stamping out a number of reprehensible practices which had crept into the game. Well-meaning as this new move was, it was unfortunately mishandled from the start. Understandably, it infuriated sports writers, who were caught off-guard like everyone else. Why, they asked, had the new directive not been announced in advance? The same question was put, for different reasons, by clubs and players. If they had known in advance, they said, their players could have been prepared for these new tactics. To this Mr Denis Follows for the Football Association, and Mr Alan Hardaker for the Football League, replied that all the referees were doing was to apply the existing rules, so that there was no need to warn anyone in advance. In any event, a copy of the Laws of Football is to be found—or should be—in the dressing-room of every League club.

There is, of course, a fallacy in this argument. Every lawyer knows that rules are not laws until they are interpreted, and the courts are well aware that, when dealing with legislation, it is what the judge says that matters. In the football world it is the referee who is the judge, on the field at any rate. Further, the rules were exactly the same before this onslaught as they were afterwards, yet the onslaught has produced a football upheaval more far-reaching than anything in the past thirty years. Something has demonstrably changed, and it can only be the referees' interpretation of the rules. Some clubs had the names of three or even more players placed in the referee's little black book in a single match. Some managers complained loudly that the new system was ruining the play of their teams. It has certainly produced some striking results from which some interesting conclusions can be drawn about the incidence of 'rough' play. For example, bookings have been higher in the Third and Fourth Divisions than in the First and Second, presumably for the reason that what the players in lower divisions lack in skill, they make up for in honest endeavour. There has also been a suspicion that players in lower divisions receive heavier sentences than those in the First.

What causes have produced this present uproar? Is it in fact true that football has become rougher and dirtier during the last decade? If it has, what are the reasons?

Those who watch football regularly, and who have done so over a long period, would probably agree that, whilst it is doubtful whether football is rougher today than it was long ago, the technique of fouling—especially to stop a skilful opponent—has certainly become a good deal subtler, and one evidence of this is that the list of injuries which any club now sustains in a season is a good deal longer than it used to be. Of course, players are more highly trained than they were previously, and the game is a good deal faster; but, in addition, the hazards are greater. An outstanding player may be 'marked' so that a deliberate attempt may be made to minimise his contribution to a game from the start, and although managers emphatically deny it, there can be no doubt that a number of them regard such action benevolently.

M

In order to introduce higher standards of conduct, the Football Association has indicated that it will hold clubs liable if their players persistently transgress, but the continuing list of bookings suggest that, as yet, the threat has not produced very positive results.

Some of the offences which earned an entry into the referee's notebook during this period were, by any standards, trifling. They have included a gesture of dissent from a referee's decision (recalling, perhaps, the 'dumb insolence' of army charge-sheets), handling the ball deliberately, and failing to retreat ten yards from the ball when a free kick is to be taken. This last offence has produced a problem, since referees were also instructed not to pace out the ten yards, as a number of them had been doing, but to stay by the ball, as this was 'more dignified'. It is not altogether surprising that there have been instances of players being booked for showing dissent at the referee's estimate.

Notwithstanding all the uproar, it is not open to doubt that once players had accustomed themselves to the new era which had dawned, the game became a good deal more agreeable to watch. It even produced international appreciation, for the Tottenham side were applauded from the field by spectators and the opposing team after a narrow win for a classic display at Turin, in a game free from incidents which had too often marred these international events.

One not unimportant factor in this 'clean-up' is the knowledge that both the Football Association and the Football League management committee stood firmly behind the referees. Referees vary a good deal in ability, even at League level. Moreover, like players, they have good games and bad ones, and when they are having a bad game, the crowd tends to get restive, so that the referee is likely to make more mistakes than he would otherwise have done. The 'new look' refereeing is as much a test of the referee as the player, but it has certainly restored authority to the referee. Gamesmanship at his expense has disappeared. On the other hand, it is also apparent that there has been variation in the attitude of referees to particular offences.

Meanwhile, a connected problem has arisen for the controlling authorities. After the passing of the Industrial Relations Act, the Minister for Sport had discussions with representatives of the Football Association, the Football League, and the Professional Footballers' Association. In the course of these he asked them to revise their disciplinary procedures to conform with the requirements of the Act, thus emphasising yet again the framework of law within which football must operate. At the conclusion of the talks, the Minister said: 'Nothing has so far been finalised, but I would like to think that football is walking along a more hopeful road. With the advent of tighter discipline in football it is more important than ever that procedures on discipline must be seen to be fair. Professional players must feel confident that the punishments to which they are exposed are fair and uniform and that they have the chance to appeal against them if they are not.'

It has been suggested by some that this means that players will have the right to be legally represented; but this is by no means the case. Many domestic tribunals (and football tribunals are, in this sense, 'domestic') do not permit legal representation. On the other hand, it would be unwise for the Association and the League to establish appeal tribunals which do not include experienced lawyers, for the pitfalls are now many, especially since the Industrial Relations Act. What is likely to be the most far-reaching effect of all is that if it is felt that in the domestic proceedings, whether at the hearing or at the appeal, there has been a failure to meet the requirements of natural justice, there may be a further appeal on this ground, exactly as there are frequently from the decisions of other domestic tribunals.

So far the evidence is that the disciplinary commissions have acted with fairness, and with apparent leniency, although one leading sports writer has suggested that they are really applying two separate standards to the greatly-increasing number of cases which come before them. If, he suggested, the player committed a foul which would have led to a booking previously, then he incurs a penalty. If his offence was simply the consequence of the instructions to referees, then in general no further action was taken.

It is clear that some aspects of this new policy will remain controversial for some time to come, and it has been suggested that there should be regular meetings between players, referees, and club representatives. These have not yet been organised, but the suggestion ought not to be forgotten. So far as players themselves are concerned, the overwhelming majority much prefer the new system to the bad old days. There is, however, one aspect of the matter which has not yet attracted attention. All the 'bookings' by referees, with the subsequent hearings, are recorded by the Football Association and the Football League. It will certainly be a guide to the players who are persistent offenders and to clubs who tolerate foul play. Accordingly there may be a day of reckoning for such clubs also. Before the opening of the 1971-72 season, representatives of and managers of eight League clubs with the worst players' records met the disciplinary committee and were asked to improve them. Few would question that such action is overdue, for it is well-known that some directors and managers have pursued a win-at-any-cost policy, to the detriment of the game as a whole, although there has always been power to reach them. Rule 36 (a) of the rules of the Football Association provides—'Every association or club is responsible for the actions of its players.'

It is not at all clear whether the attack on rough play has had any influence on the behaviour of crowds. After the first weeks of the season, spectators appeared to accept the new approach as a matter of course, and since there were no longer angry scenes between players, or between players and referee, there were correspondingly fewer outbreaks of abuse from the terraces. If there have appeared to be fewer scuffles on the terraces, it may be due (as many sports writers have suggested) to better behaviour on the field of play, or it may be the result of additional safety measures taken by the clubs, or finally it may be the result of the heavy penalties imposed on Leeds United and Manchester United, whose grounds were closed for a period at the opening of the 1971-72 season.

What has not been eliminated from the scene is the deliberate viciousness of groups of organised vandals arising out of the assembly of crowds to watch League matches. Indeed, the indications are that the evil is spreading, in spite of the increased severity with which magistrates now view the destruction for which the vandals are responsible, and which is in no way the consequence of excitement arising from the game. A very large number of towns in which important League matches are played have suffered something approaching a riot after the match. Property of many kinds has been destroyed, shops have been looted, and supporters of the opposing team have been attacked and injured. Even this is by no means the extent of the vandalism. After a match at Stamford Bridge between Chelsea and the Arsenal, returning Arsenal supporters (so-called) wrecked Underground trains to such an extent that they had to be taken out of service. On other occasions, excursion trains have virtually been given over to systematic destruction, and British Rail has threatened to discontinue these trains altogether in consequence. Where this has actually taken place, main-line trains have suffered similar damage, and ordinary passengers have been placed at risk. On several occasions the coach containing the visiting team has been attacked after the match, and members of the visiting side have sustained injuries, primarily from broken glass. There can be no question that numbers of potential supporters are deterred by these outbursts of hooliganism from attending matches, and in the long run, clubs will suffer serious financial loss. Even players on the field have suffered from objects flung at them or fired from strong catapults. Amongst objects so projected have been nuts and bolts, nails and other small steel objects.

Weapons employed by the hooligans show both variety and ingenuity. Heavy nail-studded boots were first favoured, but these were easily detected when clubs exercised greater control over the admission of spectators, and after some youths had been denied admission because they were wearing them, they have become less common. On the other hand, the police have confiscated from football vandals a forbidding museum of weapons. They include razors, flick-knives, snare wire with handles at each end (presumably for strangling), powerful catapults with nuts and bolts and staples as missiles. The latter were for use against players while the game was in progress, and a number of players have already been hit by them. In a match at Leicester, in which Leicester City played Liverpool in a pre-season 'friendly', the police seized a number of umbrellas with the tips filed down to a point. This episode is instructive. Absolutely nothing was at stake in this match, so that there could be no suggestion that violence was a by-product of natural excitement, engendered by the game. The hooligans in this instance had attended the match with one object only—to commit violence.

To combat such hooliganism within the ground itself, the clubs have employed a variety of methods, including close-circuit television, crowd marshals from the supporters' club (who have also been organised by some clubs to patrol excursion trains for away matches), and spotters placed at strategic points, equipped with long-range glasses and radios. Of necessity, much of this extra protection has been supplied by the police, and it is not cheap. For a large club, the bill may now exceed £10,000 a year.

Clubs and police alike have from time to time been exasperated by the leniency shown by magistrates when the vandals are brought before them. Fines and little homilies are quite derisory in view of the disruption which is occurring, and the seriousness of what is done. Brutal assaults and stabbings are common. Sooner or later there will be homicides. There have recently been welcome, but overdue, signs that benches are taking a more serious view, and some hooligans have been sent to prison for one or two weeks. Even so, it is doubtful whether sentences of this kind will be any real deterrent. There exists a problem which is common to many footballing countries, and which is by no means confined to football crowds. It is a symptom of the progressive breakdown of public order, and gathering together to watch a football match is the occasion and not the cause of the disorder. The uninterrupted growth of violence in the modern state will, unless checked, ultimately disrupt it, and there are at present small organised groups which, either by accident or design, are making the breakdown of public order a very real possibility. The violence of small groups of hooligans in football crowds is merely one aspect of a wave of violence, of which other manifestations are an increase in homicides and violent crimes, bomb outrages on both sides of the Irish Channel, and abroad, the hijacking of aircraft, and the kidnapping and murder of politicians and diplomats.

It would therefore be wrong to asume that this is a passing phase which, so far as football clubs are concerned, can be dealt with on an emergency basis. Until modern states with their large concentrations of population within great cities have discovered the underlying causes of this anti-social behaviour and have re-moved them, club officials will need to be ceaselessly vigilant so far as their own premises are concerned. As yet, it has not been necessary to divide up the terraces with wired-off enclosures, or to raise high fences between the playing pitch and the rest of the ground, but if the situation were to deteriorate this would have to be seriously considered. Even so, it would not solve the prob-lem of violence before or (more frequently) after a match, in the vicinity of the ground or upon public transport. There are areas in the vicinity of some large grounds in which the inhabitants lock all doors and remain off the streets until the danger hour is past.

As yet the problem is being treated emotionally, rather than rationally. Since this violence is anti-social, it follows that only a period of corrective training will make an impression upon it. In the near future, this is necessarily going to receive extended con-sideration for vandals of many different kinds. There is, of course, no guarantee that even a period of corrective training will make them decent members of society once more, but if it does not, then society cannot escape considering very seriously indeed the terms on which it is going to permit the continuation of these assaults on public order.

Index